LEXINGTON
MASSACHUSETTS

LEXINGTON
MASSACHUSETTS

TREASURES FROM HISTORIC ARCHIVES

RICHARD P. KOLLEN

Charleston   London

History
PRESS

Published by The History Press
Charleston, SC 29403
www.historypress.net

Cover Image: Assorted nineteenth-century tickets and invitations to Lexington social events.

First published 2006

Manufactured in the United Kingdom

ISBN-10 1.59629.103.6
ISBN-13 978.1.59629.103.4

Library of Congress Cataloging-in-Publication Data

Kollen, Richard.
  Lexington, Massachusetts : treasures from historic archives / Richard P. Kollen.
      p. cm.
  Includes bibliographical references.
  ISBN-13: 978-1-59629-103-4 (alk. paper)
  ISBN-10: 1-59629-103-6 (alk. paper)
  1. Lexington (Mass.)--History--18th century--Sources. 2. Lexington (Mass.)--History--19th century--Sources. 3. Lexington (Mass.)--Social life and customs--Sources. 4. Lexington (Mass.)--Biography. I. Title.
  F74.L67K655 2006
  974.4'4--dc22
                    2006025273

CONTENTS

CONTENTS

INTRODUCTION

No doubt for most Americans the name Lexington, Massachusetts, immediately brings to mind the famous battle on Lexington Common on April 19, 1775. But Lexington also hosted the first teacher education institution in the United States and was the birthplace of famous Unitarian minister and abolitionist Theodore Parker. But it is not only a town's unique qualities that make studying it valuable. The commonplace can be just as engaging and usually more significant. Living in a rural town outside Boston, past Lexington residents led lives not unlike those in many similarly placed communities. Thus, in studying how Lexingtonians lived early in the nation's history, their lives can become a prism through which to examine the basic experiences of the larger society.

Documents are among the historian's most valuable tools. Not only do they reveal aspects of the past, they humanize history. As such, they can stimulate the imagination. To work with historical documents can be a heady experience. One cannot help but feel a sense of awe when holding something created two hundred years ago. The experience can transport one back in time, evoking questions—many of which cannot be answered for certain. Where did Dr. Joseph Fiske pen the reimbursement invoice for medical services rendered on April 19, 1775, and the days following the battle? What did he look like? What was he wearing? What was he thinking? So much seems lost to history because evidence no longer exists or never did exist. But much can be learned from evidence still extant. We have the invoice, and from this much can be learned.

INTRODUCTION

The historian can only base conclusions on clues left behind in the form of documents, artifacts and oral tradition. From these traces left by people who witnessed or participated in an event, the historian attempts to reconstruct the past as closely as he can. Thus, the historian becomes a detective, piecing together evidence, making educated conjectures to fill in the gaps left unsupported by direct proof. Like the detective, the historian interrogates the source, considers it and evaluates its validity. Like the detective's clues, the source's meaning becomes clearer as more becomes known about the event. Thus, understanding of context becomes critical to both sleuths. Context breathes life into these otherwise inert clues, broadening one's understanding of its meaning. Context informs one's understanding of the documents, as the document expands one's understanding of the context.

Historical documents take many forms, from letters and diaries to advertisements and engravings. Their intended audience can be private or public. Their creators are often people with an interest in presenting a certain point of view. Each of these factors can influence the message's credibility. Thus, by necessity the historian must read a document the way a detective might interview a witness to an event. Like a witness, a document invariably transmits an incomplete record, only a slice of the event that circumstance has often biased. Even factual information by necessity omits a part of the story. Consequently, even multiple documents pertaining to an event can never fully reconstruct it.

Of course, an inherent bias determines what exists in historical archives. Historian Daniel Boorstin, former librarian of Congress, calls it the "bias of survival." His idea certainly applies to local historical society archives. First, documents about or by certain families and individuals are much more available. The "important" families with a long and successful lineage tend to collect family papers as a perceived duty to posterity. Thus, documents by or about the Munroes, the Muzzeys, the Harringtons, the Robbinses and the Reeds can be found in far greater proportions than their numerical existence in the town population. People who live briefly in town or did not see fit to save family papers, perhaps due to their station in life, leave a scant paper trail. For example, Irish immigrants were a substantial presence in Lexington for whom little private evidence can be found. Shards of their lives must be traced in public legal records and vital records. But researchers looking for letters and diaries or other personal manuscript material will likely be disappointed.

Second, documents concerning events considered important by the preservers, according to the values of the time, have a high probability of being preserved. Obviously, the Battle of Lexington has value according to past and present values. But many activities of interest today leave historians scrambling to find material. Race, gender and class are hot topics in the field today. A black presence must be found in public records. Far fewer women's papers are kept, unless they became famous writers or were married to someone famous and are part of a larger collection of the husband's papers. The activities of farmers are not well documented in manuscript material because the activity was deemed so commonplace as to not be worthy of note.

This book is a collection of essays that closely examine documents from Lexington's early past. It began as a series of newspaper articles for the *Lexington Minuteman*. The collection features documents dealing with both the unique and the commonplace. Each essay focuses on one document, parsing its language, interpreting its meaning and assessing its significance. In addition, I place the documents within their historical context. Essentially, the documents become springboards to address some aspect of Lexington's and America's history. In so doing I hope to underscore their importance not only to local history, but also to the nation's traditions. I also attempt in many essays to make a present-day connection, to show the significance of the topic to contemporary society.

The book is organized according to three basic and timeless categories— matters of home and community, matters of finance and matters of war. Some documents fit into more than one category, so I made an arbitrary choice. In selecting these documents I tried to reflect the variety of forms documents can take. Absent a linear narrative, the reader may dip into it at any point. Some characters and threads are woven throughout, and have been cross-referenced. All the documents came from the vault holding these treasures: the archives of the Lexington Historical Society. I thank the Society for its continued support for my projects. I also thank Bill Poole for advice on several of the essays.

MATTERS OF
HOME AND
COMMUNITY

This may Certify whome it may Concern that a Purpose of marriage Between Stephen Robbins and Sarah Wootton both of Lexington have been entred and published as the Law Directs———

Lexington June: 19: 1754

Att.r Isaac Bowman Town Clerk

1676

These may Certify whom it May Concern that Mr Jonas Meriam & Mrs Sarah Winship both of Lexington have been Entered & Published in Lexington as the Law Directs in order to Marriage

Lexington February y.e 27: 1758

Thaddeus Bowman Town Clerk

1677

These may Certifie whome it may Concern that the Purpose & Intention of marriage Betwixt Thomas Fessenden & Elizebeth Apthorp have Been published in Lexington as y.e Law Directs,

P.r Benja Brown
Town Cler

Lexington Feb: y.e 7.th 1765

1679

MARRIAGE BANNS
1754, 1765, 1769

M arriage has been a hot topic in Massachusetts the past few years. When the Massachusetts Supreme Judicial Court granted the right of same-sex couples to acquire marriage licenses in 2004, it set off a firestorm of debate. Some politicians have advocated civil union as a compromise position. Interestingly, the history of the civil union in Massachusetts reaches back to the Commonwealth's origin as a colony. Puritans believed marriage to be a civil union and not a sacrament; only the colonial government of Massachusetts Bay regulated marriage. Although marriage licenses had not yet evolved, their earliest forerunners were called banns. The couple had to conform to the legal requirements of marriage banns before they could marry.

The Church of England, like the Catholic Church, believed in marriage as a sacrament. In England, the king stood as the head of the Church with legal authority over all religious matters, including marriage. The Puritans dissented from this in England and transplanted their beliefs to New England. Massachusetts Bay law made marriage a civil institution by separating it from the realm of church authority. As such the ceremony took place before a magistrate, not clergy. Since New England Puritans saw the union as marriage covenant and not a sacrament, it could be ended more easily—although divorce was by no means common. A case in point, early Lexington First Parish records make no mention of marriages performed by ministers. In contrast, Anglican Church weddings were recorded in church records but did not require reporting to civil authorities.

The legal first step to matrimony is shown here. The town clerk states that the couple's intentions were "entered and published as the law directs."

Legally, these marriage banns must be publicly announced at Sunday meeting and posted on the meetinghouse door, thus published, for three consecutive weeks, before any wedding. The three marriage banns shown here were probably duplicated for posting. With some exceptions, couples violating this law could be punished for "disorderly marriage." Banns provided an opportunity for any person to object to the marriage. This assured no legal entanglement existed to prevent the marriage, such as a prospective spouse being already married.

The personal information revealed on these records conforms to patterns in mid-eighteenth century New England that historians have discovered through statistical analyses. First, the age of spouses, usually ten years after puberty, tended to be older than in England. Not as class-bound as the mother country, New England offered more opportunity for young men; thus, prospective grooms usually waited until they had acquired the resources for self-sufficiency. This involved acquiring land, learning a trade or establishing a profitable business. But marry New England men and women did—98 percent for men and 95 percent for women. Contrast that with only about 73 percent of their English cousins. Stephen Robbins was twenty-four at marriage in 1754 while Sarah Wooten's age is not known. Joshua Underwood was forty years old in 1765, likely his second marriage, while Abigail Stone's age is not known. Thomas Fessenden was twenty-seven in 1769 and Elizabeth Apthorpe was twenty-one.

When combined with the town's vital records, these marriage banns also reflect a common New England "dating" behavior practiced at the time. Historians estimate by the middle of the eighteenth century that 20 to 30 percent of brides took their wedding vows already pregnant. Many laymen with a cursory knowledge of New Englanders of Puritan stock stereotype them as prudish. They were not Victorians. As the colonies approached the Revolution, it became customary for premarital sexual activity to ensue, if the couple had become serious enough that marriage was assured. In fact, it has been estimated that fully one-third of the New England brides were "with child" as the Revolution approached. This can easily be discerned by comparing wedding date with birth date of the first child. A child born less than nine months after the wedding even had a name in the culture—an "early baby." The community attached no stigma to pregnancy before marriage at the time (unless of course the woman was not betrothed to the father). That value system changed in the nineteenth century. Of our three couples considered here, two of the brides, Sarah Wooten and Elizabeth Apthorpe, stood for their wedding four months pregnant. Abigail Stone's status is inconclusive because no birth date can be found for her first child, only a baptism date considerably later than her second born.

First Parish records document quite a few married couples who confessed to fornication. They were not confessing to sex outside their marriage with another, but to sex with each other before their marriage. This they seemed to do before a child's baptism. It seemed to clear the way for it. That they made these confessions publicly before the congregation serves as further evidence that colonial sensibilities were not shocked by such behavior.

Women and their husbands understood the dangers of childbirth during the colonial era, fearing its prospect. It made the pregnancy a mixed blessing. For two of the three women named in these banns, these fears were realized. In 1766 Abigail (Stone) Underwood died bearing her second child, who also did not survive. Elizabeth (Apthorpe) Fessenden met the same fate in 1775 while having her second child. Sarah (Wooten) Robbins did survive to live a long life. While her age is not known, she died in 1791, having birthed eleven children while being married for thirty-seven years. Her son Stephen and grandson Eli become leading citizens in East Lexington, establishing a fur dressing business and owning much of the village's land.

Thomas Fessenden remarried two years after his first wife died. The remarriage rates for men tended to be significantly higher than for women in New England, since widows outnumbered widowers. Although not the case here, a fast courtship and marriage was typical. The realities Thomas faced with two children with a household to run made marriage a practical, if not romantic, concern. He had five more children from his second wife, Lucy Lee of Concord. For widower Joshua Underwood, it is likely he remarried. A note in the genealogies of Charles Hudson's *History of Lexington VII* notes that a Joshua Underwood of West Cambridge (Arlington) married an Elizabeth Russell of Lexington in 1771. If he is the same person, he waited five years after the death of his first wife.

The legal sanction marriage banns gave a marriage remains at the root of the same-sex marriage debate today. For the Robbinses, the Underwoods and the Fessendens, no one stood in the way.

By His EXCELLENCY

FRANCIS BERNARD, Esq;

CAPTAIN-GENERAL and Governor in Chief, in and over His Majesty's Province of the MASSACHUSETTS-BAY in NEW-ENGLAND, and Vice-Admiral of the same.

A PROCLAMATION

For a Thanksgiving.

HAVING received His Majesty's Commands to appoint a Day of Thanksgiving to be observed by His good Subjects under this Government on the happy Conclusion of the Peace, I take the earliest Opportunity to execute the same, as I am convinced that such Order will be most chearfully received and religiously obeyed by this his most loyal and dutiful People. It cannot but be remembered how often We have humbled ourselves before GOD in the Time of Danger, what frequent Occasions We have had to be thankful to Him for particular Successes, and how earnest we have been to implore His Favour to bring the War to an happy Conclusion : When therefore He hath been graciously pleased to grant Us not only all that We could ask, but much more, more even than We could expect or hope ; what Bounds can be set to our grateful Adoration of the Divine Providence ? Wherefore I have appointed, and in Obedience to His Majesty's Commands, and with the Advice of His Council, I do hereby appoint *Thursday* the Eleventh Day of *August* next ensuing, to be a Day of *Public Prayer and Thanksgiving*, to return Thanks to Almighty GOD for His great Mercies in conducting us through this long, bloody and expensive War unto an honorable, advantageous, and, as We may well hope, a lasting Peace. And I do appoint the said Day to be a Day of *Public Worship*, and order that no servile Labour be permitted on the same.

GIVEN at the Council-Chamber in Boston, *the Twenty-seventh Day of* July, 1763, *in the Third Year of the Reign of our Sovereign Lord* GEORGE *the Third, by the Grace of* GOD, *of* Great-Britain, France *and* Ireland, KING, *Defender of the Faith,* &c.

By His Excellency's Command,
A. OLIVER, Sec'ry.

Fra. Bernard.

GOD Save the KING.

THANKSGIVING PROCLAMATION, 1763

Regardless of one's position on the war with Iraq, sensible Americans approached it with a sense of dread. They understood all too well the inevitable loss of lives and treasure associated with war. As this war continues, one thing is certain—Americans will be grateful for its end. February 10, 1763, marked the signing of a treaty ending a North American war after nine years of fighting. The American part of the Seven Years' War, pitting the British against the French and its Indian allies, actually was the last in a series of wars involving these opponents. It resulted in France's loss of virtually all claims to the continent, leaving Britain in control of most of North America. American colonists, as British citizens, fought on the side of their mother country, usually as a separate provincial force. The colonies typically bore an economic burden and loss of life. Understandably, war's end brought celebration and relief.

On July 27, 1763, King George III ordered that a day of thanksgiving be observed in the American colonies to properly thank God for a "happy Conclusion of the Peace." With the imprimatur of King George III's seal heading the page, Massachusetts Governor Francis Bernard responded with this proclamation. He chose Thursday, August 11 for the occasion and directed that it be a "Day of Public Worship," ordering that no "servile Labor be permitted."

Close inspection of the document reveals that ink has leaked through from the reverse side in the right margin. If held to a mirror, it becomes clear that the proclamation was addressed to Reverend Jonas Clarke, the logical person to minister a day of thanksgiving. Not regularly observed in

November until the second half of the nineteenth century, thanksgiving days were not predetermined. The church believed occasions suitable for giving thanks to be bestowed by God. Given life's unpredictability, predetermined days on a calendar made little sense. The king viewed the end of this costly war as a worthy occasion for expressing gratitude to God.

As part of the proclamation, Governor Bernard noted that the war was "long, bloody and expensive." Lexington men filled many muster rolls from 1755 to 1763, fighting on battlefields such as Louisburg, Quebec, Crown Point and Ticonderoga. Some, such as Edmund Monroe, served with the famous Roger's Rangers, frontiersmen known for ranging in the wilderness and functioning as the eyes and ears of the British army. In all, over one hundred men from the town served in the final French war. On April 19, 1775, twenty-five to thirty still lived in Lexington with many present on the Common. Two were commissioned officers, Lieutenant Edmund Monroe and Ensign Robert Monroe.

For young men in their early twenties, often relegated to laboring while awaiting their inheritance and opportunity to start out on their own, enlistment provided distinct advantages. Terms of services were short, usually six to eight months, and the pay was relatively high for the provincial army. A break from routine and the capital to start out without waiting for parental support led many to join, such as Benjamin Merriam, age twenty, and Jeremiah Bridge, age twenty-three. Both married soon after service.

The Lexington homefront felt the financial pinch as the Commonwealth raised taxes repeatedly to pay for the provincial's side of the war. That economic hard times hit home can be seen in the number of times town meeting voted to "sink" or lower the taxes on individuals to help them pay. Sometimes these individuals had just returned from the war; others seemed to need some kind of relief. The number of these citizens increased markedly during the war.

In addition, an unusual event for a mid-eighteenth-century Congregational community occurred as a byproduct of the war. The Commonwealth of Massachusetts sent a French Catholic family to board in Lexington. While anti-Catholic animosity had tempered a bit by 1755, Roman Catholics still could not freely exercise their religion and it remained a capital offense for a Catholic priest to enter Massachusetts. Furthermore, the war had elevated an omnipresent anti-Catholic prejudice.

Why was the family sent here? A victory in Nova Scotia in 1755 led to the forced removal of the French civilians who had previously sworn an oath of neutrality in case of war between Britain and France. When the British entered Nova Scotia, they demanded the Acadians swear a new stronger oath requiring them to take up arms against the French, rendering them subjects of the British king. They refused. Feared as a security risk, these Acadians were taken from their homes, their houses and barns were burned and they were deported to the mainland colonies. Boston received about one thousand Acadians in November, which the General Court distributed among the surrounding towns. According to the Massachusetts General Court, the Acadian exiles fell under the provincial poor laws. Towns were required to house and feed them in the winter, but they must be self-supporting soon after or be treated as paupers. Children could be bound out, separating them from parents.

August Hibbert, his wife and boy arrived in Lexington on December 1, 1755. What their lives were like is hard to imagine. Town records show they were cared for responsibly. The town paid reimbursement to individuals who boarded them for a time or provided necessary items. Items such as shoes, cords of wood, pork and barrels of cider show up in town records as paid for by the town. By 1757, without the expected reimbursement from the Commonwealth or from England forthcoming, and with tightening economic conditions, the Hibberts' allowance grew more meager. Finally, they were treated as paupers. While the province later provided some reimbursement, the town constable brought the Hibberts to Groton in 1761, whose authorities subsequently sent them to Waltham.

With the end of the war, the citizens of Lexington were thankful indeed. It is one of the realities of the Iraq war that Lexingtonians, 240 years later, can understand how they felt.

1 — clear & pleasant. went to Hopkinton

2 — pleasant. — Apprizing my Father's Estate.

3 — cloudy, rain. (Mrs Sinkord's Dan'l Jr. died

4 — pleasant. (also Mr David Sinkords Child died at

5 — ditto. returned Home.

6 — ditto.

7 — cloudy, rain. at Waltham.

8 — cloudy, rain. at Night rain. Mr Andrew

9 — ditto. Elener Phe died. (Pashe died.

10 — clears off pleasant. went to Mr Cooks.

11 — clear, Windy S. West. at Night rain.

12 — clears off. windy.

13 — clear, cool. Night

14 — Pleasant. at Lexington. cloudy at y

15 — ditto.

16 — cloudy, rain, a N.E. Storm.

17 — clears off pleasant. I preached.

18 — pleasant. ∫Massacre in Lexington & y

19 — ditto. A cture, to commemorate the y

20 — clear, cool. Rain from

21 — pleasant. at Lexington. at Night cloudy
Child died

22 — cloudy, — small Showers. Mr Robinson's
went to Boston

23 — clear, cold, windy. Broth Bowes & Family

24 — pleasant — Mr Moore ploughed the Garden

25 — warm, pleasant. went to Hopkinton.

26 — very warm. P.M. thun. Showers.

27 — clear, pleasant. returned with Trunks &c

28 — very pleasant. at Lexington.

29 — ditto. ∫ Sowed Rye

30 — cloudy, rain. Mr Marrett here

Hon. Madm Lydia Hancock died at
Fairfield, April 25 1776. suddenly! —

A PAGE FROM REVEREND JONAS CLARKE'S ALMANAC DIARY 1776

Do not expect to learn about Reverend Jonas Clarke's innermost thoughts and feelings when reading his diary. Notwithstanding any predilection he might have had to use a diary for such purposes, the almanac diary format precludes thoughtful, extended entries. An almanac diary, as shown here, places on a single page all days of a month, thus limiting space for day-to-day musings. Still Clarke's almanac diary remains a singularly useful source because it records the activities of a minister, patriot and farmer in Lexington.

This page documents April 1776. When examining Clarke's daily records, three threads emerge. The prevalence of death seems unavoidable. The number of deaths in this and the preceding months appears unusually high, even for the era, when compared to his entries in other years. Clarke's role as minister, of course, placed him at the center of mourning those who pass from this life. He does not refer to the reason for the spike in mortality rate, so one is left to speculate. Smallpox had begun to infect the Boston area early in 1776. When the British left Boston in March, they left a city wracked with the disease. American residents' isolation from Europe for generations made them far more susceptible to smallpox than the British army, whose systems had acquired tolerance. Elizabeth Fenn in *Pox Americana: The Great Smallpox Epidemic of 1775–82* writes that many in the Continental Army who attempted to invade Canada in May 1776 suffered from smallpox. Whether smallpox can account for the increase in Lexington's death rate remains unknown. But later in the year Clarke's diary entries make clear that smallpox had by then arrived in Lexington. On December 20, 1776,

Clarke had himself and his family inoculated. The subsequent illness that sometimes ensued kept Clarke from the pulpit for two Sundays in January 1777. His family took sick also, but all survived the inoculation.

Two deaths mentioned in April happened outside Lexington but hit even closer to home. Clarke's father had died at seventy-one in June 1775, two weeks after the death of his mother. The minister spent time in early April tending to his father's affairs in Hopkinton, Massachusetts. He seemed to have acquired some moveable property as a result, since later in April he returned from Hopkinton "with trunks, etc." Clarke's frequent visits to other towns reveals a mobility not often ascribed to this time and place.

Lydia Hancock died "Suddenly!" in Fairfield, Connecticut, on April 25. Word of her death reached Clarke five days later. The previous year, Lydia Hancock had slept in the parsonage the night Paul Revere raised his alarm. On that night she served as chaperone since Dorothy Quincy had joined her fiancé John Hancock. As John's aunt, she was also Clarke's relation by marriage. Although elderly, her death seems to have surprised Clarke.

The theme of death relates to another thread: memories of the previous April day in 1775 that left ten Lexingtonians dead. The Battle of Lexington seemed to have begun a movement toward independence. But in April 1776 the formal Declaration of Independence still remained a couple months away. Clarke, as minister, preached the first anniversary sermon on April 19, 1776, the one year anniversary "to commemorate the massacre in Lexington." This began a tradition of anniversary sermons that continued for years by other ministers. That the town minister stood at the center of the commemoration sermon makes sense. Clarke also stood at the center of events that day, lending more than moral support. Not only was Clarke the most important political figure in Lexington, he hosted John Hancock and Sam Adams for several days before April 19, 1775. Paul Revere headed to his parsonage as soon as he arrived in Lexington. Revere had been at the parsonage several days earlier to confer with Adams and Hancock.

Clarke subtitles his anniversary sermon "To Commemorate, the MURDER, BLOODSHED and commencement of hostilities between Great Britain and America." He begins the sermon with Joel 3: 19–21, using Egypt's oppression of the Israelites as entrée to considering later cases of peoples who abandoned an oppressive government. Then he traces the history of American grievances. In describing the events of April 19, Clarke lays the blame entirely on the British. He says, "They approach with the morning's light; and more like murderers and cutthroats than the troops of a Christian king." Clarke predicts that from the event in Lexington will "be dated in future history, the LIBERTY or SLAVERY of the AMERICAN WORLD, according as a sovereign God shall see fit to smile, or frown upon the interesting cause, in which we are engaged."

But like those who stood on the Common that day, Clarke was also a farmer. His fifty-acre farm extended all the way down Hancock Street toward the Common to include the land that Lexington Academy bought and where Masonic Temple now stands. His daily notes, if perused over the years, reveal farming's seasonal cycle. Annually Clarke began plowing and planting in April. He received help this year: "Mr. Moore ploughed the garden." Most other years he did the work himself.

Clarke's diary page records that he "sowed rye." Exactly three months later on July 30 he "reaped rye." Grains provided the staple food for colonial farmers. Lexington farmers' probate inventories reveal supplies of barley, oats, wheat and rye. Planting was a May–June activity for certain vegetables such as potatoes. But he records sowing rye in July and wheat in November. Clarke also "set out" tobacco plants one year, an experiment that he did not continue.

The earliest colonists in Massachusetts Bay transplanted the English practice of mixed husbandry—a marriage of herding and tillage. Once woods were cleared, the terrain of eastern Massachusetts proved quite similar to that most emigrants left behind in the East Anglia region of England, although existing in a harsher climate. This form of husbandry combined raising livestock with growing grains, fruits and vegetables. The paucity of fertile tracks of land in the region required these be integrated into a productive system. Farmers used some land for tillage and other for pasture to graze livestock, and meadows produced hay for fodder. Orchards, most commonly made up of apple trees, provided an essential complement to early Massachusetts's settlers' subsistence.

Virtually all Lexington probate inventories include cider presses and cider barrels. Clarke annually reports making cider in November and December to store for the winter in his barrels. Apples mature in the fall and can be stored in barrels for the winter. On October 6, 1774, Clarke records, "Gathering winter apples." Usually farmers slaughtered livestock during the winter months, when they could best be preserved. Clarke participated in this seasonal ritual when he "killed the ox" on December 26, 1775. Two weeks later he killed a calf.

One can only infer Clarke's feelings about these events, a disappointment to twenty-first-century sensibilities. But even the sparsely detailed recordings offer a window into eighteenth-century life.

RESIDENCE OF STEPHEN ROBBINS,

Erected about 1720.

ENGRAVING OF THE ROBBINS HOMESTEAD, 1810

As one travels down Massachusetts Avenue toward Arlington, perhaps stopping at the traffic lights along the way, one might do a little time traveling. Place yourself on the same road going in the same direction in 1810. Near the junction of Pleasant Street, look to the left and imagine the idyllic scene depicted in the engraving shown here. This is the homestead of the estimable Stephen Robbins Jr., patriarch of East Lexington's "First Family."

In the late 1700s Robbins established himself as proprietor of the first fur-dressing enterprise in East Lexington. Although he later acquired several competitors in the village, Robbins's business was undoubtedly the largest in scale, growing to over one hundred employees after turning over the operation to his son, Eli. Fur-dressing manufacturers produced fur capes, muffs, fur-lined boots, gloves and other products from pelts. Robbins, who also owned a dry goods store, at first exchanged West India goods for pelts. He paid his workers in goods from the store. Robbins's account books show he and his sons ranging outside the state into New York and even Canada to purchase bear and sable pelts. He regularly traveled to Boston to buy his West India goods. Locally, he purchased deer, fox and rabbit pelts. Robbins even manufactured and sold "pole cat" muffs and tippets, or stoles.

Stephen Robbins married Abigail Winship, of Lexington, in 1779. The Winship family owned a sawmill closer to the Arlington or West Cambridge line. Robbins ran the Winship sawmill along with a spice and gristmill in other locations. He owned vast tracts of land in the East Village full of peat and wood, including nearly the entire Great Meadow. Due to Stephen Robbins's entrepreneurial success, the Robbins family became the most prominent family in the village for generations. Among the family's many benefactions, Stephen donated the land for the meetinghouse, now Follen Church. His son Eli continued the Robbins family contributions to making East Village a vibrant community in the early nineteenth century.

Sixteen-year-old Caira Robbins, his daughter, probably produced a watercolor that provided the basis for this engraving of Stephen Robbins's homestead in 1810. The Robbins papers contain several Caira Robbins watercolors. Although this engraving is not among them, it is drawn in similar style. The engraving shows the house from the Massachusetts Avenue side, where it stood for most of its existence, near the junction of Pleasant Street, at number 669. Trees, probably elm, figure prominently in the engraving, lending it the air of a country estate. It is well known that Stephen and Eli planted elm trees along Massachusetts Avenue, and probably on their properties. Dutch elm disease has since destroyed them.

While the engraving's caption dates the house's construction at 1720, evidence indicates that it was built four years earlier. This evidence comes in the form of the numeral 1716 surviving on a wall below eight coats of paint. The colonial style house, with its saltbox roof, seems to be flanked on the left by outbuildings or stables. At the time the roof sloped very low in the back. Inside a fireplace graced each of the eight rooms, but the rooms in the rear were necessarily made smaller by the sloped roof. A hay wagon passes in front toward Arlington, while a one-horse chaise canters toward the center village.

George O. Smith wrote in the *Proceedings of the Lexington Historical Society Proceedings V. II* that Stephen Robbins "owned a white horse that was constantly harnessed to a bellows-topped chaise, ready to take him to the various places where his work was being carried on." The two-wheeled single-horse vehicle depicted here was called the Boston chaise, a very popular vehicle in the early 1800s. It featured wood and leather springing to enable the driver to weather the rough backcountry roads. Also called the bellows-topped chaise, as Smith referred to it, its retractable leather top allowed the rider to enjoy favorable weather.

The Robbins family occupied the house for 161 years. Abigail and Stephen Robbins first occupied the house by leasing it from Joseph Robinson in 1781, two years after their marriage. Stephen lived there for the rest of his life until 1847, as did Abigail until 1850. Then their daughter Caira moved in to occupy the house until her death in 1881. Stephen's granddaughter, Mrs. Ellen Robbins Stone, then lived there until 1890. Her daughter Miss Ellen Stone had been born in the house in 1854 and remained there until her passing in 1944. Soon events transpired to place the survival of the house in jeopardy. It seemed destined to be torn down for the lot. Fortunately, Helen

Potter purchased it for $500 and moved it in 1948, a *Christian Science Monitor* article notes, thirty-five-ton chimney and all, one mile toward Lexington center, to number 1295. The move cost $3,300.

By the date of the engraving, Stephen had turned over the fur-dressing enterprise to his son Eli in 1809, but records show he stayed involved. Once he "retired," Stephen sold wood and peat, or "turf" as he called it. In the middle of Great Meadow stood three storage sheds to hold peat. Wood was stacked at the Robbins house. Albert Bryant remembers in the same *Proceedings* volume, "wood by the hundred cords was stacked in front of his house, around his buildings and on the road side." The leaves on the trees in the engraving show it not to be the season when stacks of wood would be visible. He also continued to run the Winship sawmill. Smith remembers Stephen Robbins Jr. as an eccentric. This became an acknowledged Robbins trait over the course of a generation. A throwback, Robbins invariably wore a long coat, knee breeches and long stockings long after pants became the style. He also continued to wear his hair in a queue. Albert Bryant never saw him without a hat, inside or outside the house. According to Bryant, a person who knocked on Robbins's door would be greeted by the command, "Walk." Once inside the visitor would be told, "Sit." Meanwhile, Robbins never rose from his traditional seat near the fireplace.

As you come out of your reverie and resume life in traffic on Massachusetts Avenue, understand that a time has passed never to return. The village could not have been called sleepy, for too much activity would belie that description. But it was a pace much slower and more relaxed—a time to which we can never return.

ADMIT *Miss Fanny Harrington*

TO THE BALL AT MUNROE'S HALL, IN
LEXINGTON, ON *Monday the 29 of February*
at five o'clock P.M.

JONAS MUNROE,
BENJ. O. WELLINGTON, } Managers.
JOHN MILLIKEN,

1808

Floor Managers,

Nath'l Garmon,
H. A. Wellington,
F. H. Kneeland,
N. Jenney.
George Flint,
Edwin Spaulding

Music, Bond's Band.

FIVE PIECES.

A. B. MORSS, PR., BOSTON,

SOCIAL PARTY,

AT

CUTLER'S HOTEL,

EAST LEXINGTON,

Wednesday Evening,

Jan. 30, 1867.

Order of Dances,

March and Sicilian Circle.

1	Quadrille.	We meet again.
2	Quadrille.	Welcome all.
3	Contra,	Merry Dance.
4	Quadrille.	Caledonia.
5	Quadrille.	Ladies' Choice.

Waltz, Schottische, Polka.

6	Quadrille.	Sleigh Bells.
7	Quadrille,	Lancers.
8	Polka Quadrille,	Kind Friends.
9	Quadrille,	Band's Choice.
10	Quadrille,	Military.

INTERMISSION AND SUPPER.

Waltz, Esmeralda, Polka, Galop.

11	Quadrille,	Mocking Bird.
12	Contra,	Chorus Jig.
13	Quadrille,	Surprise.
14	Quadrille,	Portland Fancy.
15	Contra,	Hull's Victory.

Schottische, Varsovienne.

16	Quadrille,	Rock Point.
17	Quadrille,	Out of town Friends.
18	Contra,	Virginia Reel.
19	Quadrille,	Medley.
20	Quadrille,	All going Home.

Engagements.

1	
2	
3	Kneeland
4	
5	
6	
7	
8	
9	
10	
11	
12	Charlie Butterfield
13	
14	
15	
16	
17	
18	
19	Charlie Butterfield
20	

TICKET TO A DANCE, 1808 AND DANCE CARD, 1867

"There is nothing to do in this town!" is a popular refrain among young people in Lexington today. If true, they can at least take comfort in the fact that ease of transportation places them within minutes of the city or another more promising location. In the early nineteenth century, most Lexingtonians stayed close to home for their entertainment venues by necessity—and they seemed to like it.

At one point as many as twelve taverns offered residents and travelers opportunities to gather. Taverns prospered when livestock and carts of produce traveled down Main Street, now Massachusetts Avenue, on the way to the markets of Boston and the stockyards of Brighton. In the center village teamsters enjoyed Dudley Tavern near the Common for dinner. Buckman Tavern more often served travelers on stagecoach. On the present site of CVS, Monument House did the briskest business. Further east along Massachusetts Avenue, Munroe Tavern offered the last stop before the cattle and sheep driven from New Hampshire, Vermont and Canada reached Brighton. Drovers planned their itinerary so that they reached Munroe on Saturday. There they remained until Monday to rest their stock to present its best appearance upon arrival at the stockyards. Proprietor Jonas Munroe charged twenty-five cents per head for cattle and five or ten cents for sheep to graze on his adjoining farm. During peak times hundreds of cattle and sheep used the Munroe facilities each week, earning Jonas a tidy sum.

Taverns became integral to local social life, serving as an entertainment venue for town-wide events. Monument House and Munroe Tavern hosted public dinners and balls. The invitation to a ball at Munroe's, shown here, reveals some interesting information about these events. First, the dance was held on Monday, rather than on a weekend. In this pre-industrial society the demarcation between workday and leisure days was not as clear—except for the Sabbath. More important, however, was the season. Most evidence of dances in town show dances scheduled during the winter months, rather than the more busy months for farmers. This was fortunate because a town tradition existed, according to Edward Bliss in the *Proceedings of the Lexington Historical Society, Vol. 1*, that the dancing must end twelve hours after it began. A typical start time was 5:00 p.m., as it states on the Munroe ticket. If tradition prevailed, the dance continued until 5:00 a.m.

Sixteen-year-old Fanny Harrington owned the ticket. In 1820 she married Horace Skilton of Bedford and they had four children together. Given the twelve-year gap between the dance and marriage, it is unlikely the courtship began that night. But clearly town dances offered a critical social activity for young people. A fiddler sometimes furnished the music. Peter Tulip, a poor African American farm resident, often provided the fiddling. His daughters often constituted the wait staff for these events. A story passed down recounts how at a dance in 1815 at Munroe Tavern, practical joker Jonas Munroe waxed the strings of Tulip's fiddle bow with a candle while the musician took a break. Munroe got a kick out of his practical joke when Tulip found no sound emitted from the fiddle.

What this document does not reveal, of course, is how the social structure of the town might have determined attendance. What elements of Lexington society frequented these events and who was unwelcome? Very few African Americans lived in town. Would they be welcome, if they were entertainment or waiting on tables? Irish migration to the town remained decades away. But by the 1850s and 1860s they would be a notable presence. Would they be invited?

Among the dance forms practiced in the early nineteenth century, the minuet became the most popular. It involved multiple dance partners in progression. Soon English country dances caught on—the cotillion and the quadrille. Since these were set dances, done in formations and lines, they foreshadowed the later square dance. Since these involved single partners, dance cards became a part of dance etiquette. They listed the dances scheduled for the night and provided an accompanying space for names. As a lady promised a man a dance he wrote his initial or name in the space provided. A full dance card meant quite a few partners. The card served as both a memory aid and a memento from the event. A woman wore these on her wrist. The gentleman also used dance cards to record his dance commitments. Popular indeed was the person with a full dance card—especially with a variety of partners.

Shown here are four panels of a dance card. The top shows what would have been the cover. The dance order and list of partners sits, printed on the inside, shown below that. The quadrille figured prominently in the night's dances, with a couple contra dances mixed in. The event seemed more than a dance, since a meal was served halfway though. The dance card belonged to a popular female: a man spoke for every dance that night. Charles Butterfield had three including the last two of the night. The cover shows that the event took place at Cutler's Hotel (formerly East Lexington Tavern). The hotel stood near the lower corner of Fottler Avenue, near Arlex Oil. When Lexington entered its hotel era, the name became Cutler's Hotel. It burned down in 1875.

Dancing was such a popular pastime in the United States and Europe that the job of a dance master, one who teaches dance and organizes the intricate dances at a ball, became a popular occupation. In particular dance lessons were the rage in Lexington in the mid-1820s. Among Lexingtonians, Eli Robbins, as a younger man, fancied himself a dance master, although his fur-dressing business in East Village supplied his primary source of income. Beginning in the 1830s Robbins funded the building of Robbins Hall, now the East Lexington Branch Library, among other projects. Albert Bryant remembers that Robbins had no formal background in music but could play the violin well, and could dance while playing. Robbins taught dance in Lexington and surrounding towns. Clearly he did this for the love of it. In warm weather he sat on his front step at Massachusetts Avenue serenading passersby with his violin. Eli's brother, Lot, was also a dance master as well as a penmanship teacher.

It is doubtful the children of the farming town of Lexington complained about the lack of things to do in town. Instead, they probably appreciated the diversion from work.

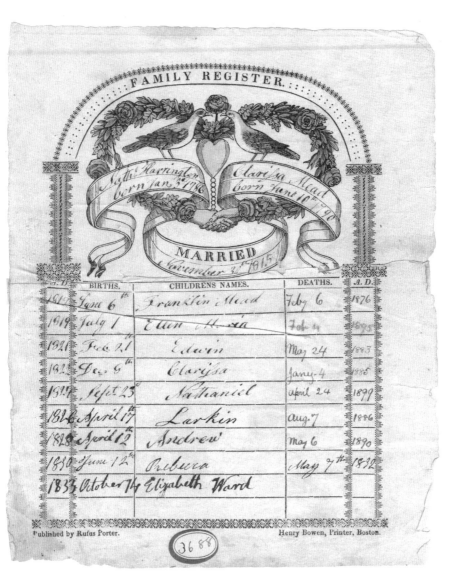

FAMILY REGISTER.

Nath Harrington
born Jan 3 1786

Clarissa Mead
born June 10th 1796

MARRIED
November 3d 1815

A.D.	BIRTHS.	CHILDRENS NAMES.	DEATHS.	A.D.
1816	June 6th	Franklin Mead	Feby 6	1876
1819	July 1	Ellen Maria	Feb 4	1895
1821	Feb 21	Edwin	May 24	1883
1823	Dec 9th	Clarissa	Jany 4	1885
1827	Sept 25	Nathaniel	April 24	1899
1826	April 17th	Larkin	Aug. 7	1886
1828	April 12th	Andrew	May 6	1890
1830	June 12th	Rebecca	May 7th	1872
1833	October 14	Elizabeth Ward		

Published by Rufus Porter. Henry Bowen, Printer, Boston.

36 88

HARRINGTON FAMILY REGISTER
1815

The process of tracing family lineages sends researchers to the National Archives branches throughout the country to search census and ship records. Public records such as these are not the only resources available to genealogists. Family registers such as the one shown here could be found hanging on walls throughout New England in the years following the Revolution. Some have found their way into local historical society archives. The Lexington Historical Society archives preserved Clarissa and Nathaniel Harrington's family register. They show their pride in family through this decorative visual.

As Peter Benes has noted in "Decorated Family Registers in New England," an article found in *The Art of Family*, family registers became popular around the time of the American Revolution and continued into the mid-nineteenth century. Unsatisfied with simply recording vital records in the family Bible, families sought a visual display to satisfy an increasing interest in genealogy. Most rejected the coat of arms or family portrait displayed prominently by wealthy families. Ultimately, decorated family registers seemed more republican in spirit. These usually included the names of the married couple with their wedding date, followed by the birth and death record of their children. One-page visual representations suitable for framing, families often displayed them in a prominent place. Some were embroidered and others lettered on paper. Sometimes children made them in school and, as their popularity increased, printers published their own versions.

The design of family registers drew on the artist's creativity, especially after private printers began to compete for sale of them. Some typical motifs recur. The marriage of the couple may be represented by two hearts or, in the case of the Harringtons', two lovebirds with a heart in the middle. Also, two hands embracing further symbolized the union sanctioned by matrimony. The family, as shown here, often formed an architectural structure with pillars. The children, it appears, provide the foundation and stability to the parental union atop the structure.

Nathaniel Harrington and Clarissa Mead grew up as neighbors in the center village in the early nineteenth century. Nathaniel lived in a house along today's Harrington Road, then Elm Street, sitting between two other Harrington homes. To its left Jonathan Harrington's house stood on the corner of Harrington Road and Bedford Street. To its right Levi Harrington's house stood next to First Parish Church once the fourth meetinghouse was built in 1846. Jonathan Harrington's house remains today, made famous as the dwelling to which Jonathan Harrington dragged himself after incurring fatal wounds during the April 19 battle on the Common. Levi Harrington built his house after the Revolutionary War. It also remains in the same location. The house that Nathaniel Harrington lived in predated the Revolution, having been built by his grandfather, Daniel Harrington, clerk of the militia. It was torn down in 1875 when the town declined an offer from the owner to sell it, leaving an empty space between the two other Harrington dwellings.

The Meads lived on the lot now occupied by Cary Memorial Library. Clarissa's grandfather, Matthew Mead, lived at the present Russell Square location on April 19, 1775. The British ransacked his house on the return to Boston. Mead claimed 101 pounds in damage to his property.

One can imagine Nathaniel traveling across the Common to visit Clarissa. In those years of limited mobility, proximity influenced marriage choices. Clarissa's sister, Martha, married Nathaniel's cousin, Nathan, and her sister, Maria, married Nathan Chandler, who lived not far away on Hancock Street. The typical marriage age at the time for women ranged from twenty to twenty-seven years old, for men from twenty-four to thirty. Marriages between the very young were rare. The man needed time to establish himself as self-supporting. Due to later marriages, a courting period of several years often preceded nuptials. Clarissa and Nathaniel may have been a couple at Lexington social events for quite a while. These probably included the balls, sleighing parties or picnics. As the register shows, the groom was twenty-nine and the bride twenty-five years old for their wedding in 1815.

When Nathaniel died at fifty-three years old in 1839, the youngest of his nine children, Elizabeth Ward, was five years old and the oldest, Franklin Mead, had just turned twenty-two. Perhaps indicative of life for a widow with children and no social safety net, Clarissa sold the contents of the house four months later. Presumably she moved in with relatives, of which there should have been many nearby, especially on the extensive Harrington side of the family. She listed items for sale in the advertisement to include household furniture as well as one swine, one horse, one ox, one beef cow, one horse cart, one ox wagon and one sleigh. Also to be sold were farmer's and mason's tools. Harrington had not been poor. He owned real estate worth $2,850 and a personal estate assessed at $670.79. In the 1851 town valuation Clarissa owned Lexington real estate worth $2,086.

A letter exists in the archives, dated May 16, 1855, from the Bureau of Pensions to Elizabeth Ward Harrington, granting bounty land to Clarissa for Nathaniel's service in the War of 1812. As a sergeant in the militia, he served for ninety-two days in the war. The government often granted bounty land rather than money for military service, since it was so plentiful. At the time the federal government created military districts in Michigan, Illinois and present-day Arkansas (then Louisiana Territory) for veterans who were promised land. Why Elizabeth made the request rather than Clarissa is not known. But the request was granted. Clarissa now owned land in a distant location.

Clarissa died twenty-six years later while living in Cambridge. She was seventy-five. If the marriage register remained in her possession until then, it appears someone else recorded the subsequent deaths of her children. Perhaps it was Elizabeth Ward Harrington, whose 1906 death while visiting Blois, France, remains unrecorded. She never married. Elizabeth is credited with providing seed money in 1904 for Lexington's Home for the Aged, today the Dana Home. Later in her life one can imagine Elizabeth's wall adorned with the register and memories of growing up in a house that skirted Lexington Common.

Harriet Munroe | 3 TERM 1834.

EXPLANATION.

t. tardy.	3. very good recitation.	*n.* noisy at school.
t. e. tardy, but excused.	2. indifferent recitation.	*i.* idle.
a. absent.	1. bad recitation.	*w.* whispering.
a. e. absent, but excused.	1-. very bad recitation.	*d.* disorderly out of school.

WEEK.	t.	t. e.	d.	a. e.	RECITATIONS.				DEMEANOR.				REMARKS.
					3.	2.	1.	1-.	w.	i.	w.	d.	
FIRST				9									Account begun on
SECOND				13									
THIRD				8									
FOURTH				10									Deportment highly creditable.
FIFTH			7										
SIXTH				12									
SEVENTH			1	14									
EIGHTH				13									
NINTH			1	14	1								
TENTH				17									Good in Arithmetic
ELEVENTH				14									Some
TWELFTH				19									Some
THIRTEENTH				12									
FOURTEENTH													
FIFTEENTH	Amount			9	155	1							Deportment and scholarship unexceptionable.
SIXTEENTH													

HARRIET MUNROE'S REPORT CARD
1834

Report cards elicit excitement and not a little trepidation among students today. The letter grades or written narratives purport to represent the sum total of the student's school performance for that particular class, despite the impossibility of that task. Early nineteenth-century report cards tended to be less specific, but they no doubt carried similar import.

Shown here is Harriet Munroe's report card for the second term in 1834. Harriet was the daughter of Jonas Munroe, proprietor of Munroe Tavern. According to the 1830 school district map, she lived within the center school district, just outside the East Lexington district. This school's lineage can be traced almost from the incorporation of the town. Lexington's first school occupied schoolhouse hill on the Common in 1716. The town replaced the building in 1761, and removed it from the Common in 1795. The Revolutionary Monument has occupied the hill since 1799. An ongoing controversy regarding the school's accessibility to the growing "country" or outlying population of children led to the onset of district schools. Three were built—one on North Hancock Street, one on Mason's Hill not far from Munroe Tavern and one in the south district.

Thus, for a time Lexington had a school system with three schoolhouses, but none in the center. In 1804 the town constructed a new twenty-two by twenty-eight-foot one-story schoolhouse once again on the Common, as three new districts were added. One school, near the juncture of Woburn and Lowell Streets, served the Scotland area. The Smith's End school stood on Concord Street, west of Waltham Street. East Village now had its own district, moving the school from Mason's Hill to a site across the street from

Follen Church. An 1821 town meeting voted to move the center school to the Massachusetts Avenue location near where the Baptist Church stands today—down the street from Harriet's father's tavern. In 1829 the school underwent expansion, building a second story to differentiate instruction between the younger and older students.

Emery Mulliken left written recollections of his early education at this schoolhouse, describing the classroom on the first floor. He writes that upon entering the school, stacks of wood and student coats filled much of the vestibule. At the front of the single schoolroom stood "a large box stove," while on the opposite side the teacher's elevated desk stood "like the old fashioned church pulpit." Fourteen-inch wide planks of wood along the two remaining sides, with spaces for books underneath, served as student desks. The "scholars" sat on a narrower plank set lower. Five rows of desks extended to the walls, each at a higher elevation. Boys and girls sat on opposite sides of the room. To serve as a recitation area, about one-third of the room was left vacant. It is here that a younger Harriet probably recited her lessons, which were graded on report cards.

At seventeen Harriet would have been among the older students in the class taught on the second floor. Since Emery Mulliken himself graduated at nineteen years old, the advanced age was by no means unique. Rewards of Merit sent home to Harriet's parents date from ten years earlier, so she had attended school most of her life. Mulliken remembers that a male teacher taught the older "scholars" on the second floor. Generally, older students attended the winter term only. During the summer term, these valuable hands were needed on the farm, leaving only the younger students. The second term referred to on the report card was probably the winter term.

Many male teachers at the time often taught school in the winter term while working their way through college. For example, Theodore Parker taught at Lexington's north district school while attending Harvard. Others chose teaching as a career. Charles Tidd, who taught at the east district school, fell into that category. He taught for thirty years while serving on the school committee for some of that time. Women usually taught the younger children, especially during the summer term, until marriage. They then had to give up their positions. Mulliken mentions Abby Anne Muzzey as a teacher he remembered fondly. She married William Brigham in 1834. In most cases "teaching" was too professional a term to ascribe to what they did. With no training, schoolmasters often referred to their occupation as "keeping school" rather than teaching.

The structure of a report card can offer a window into a school's value system. On this particular report card one immediately notices grades only for recitation, without indicating which subjects. With a multiplicity of ages and subjects to manage, this may have been the most practical method of evaluation. Harriet achieved the highest score almost without exception. Of the four possible "grades" available it is interesting to note that only one carries a positive description. Raising the self-esteem of students in Harriet's time was not a priority. Summative comments at the end of the term state that Harriet's "comportment and scholarship was unexceptionable." Her 155 recitations out of 156 opportunities were "very good." Earlier in her school career she drew praise such as "a fine little scholar" with regular Rewards of Merit send home. The faint praise she received at seventeen may be a function of the teacher's personality or a change in her attitude. She missed seven excused days of school. It seems she was quite sick during the fifth week.

With well-behaved children a parental goal at the time, behavior became an important category. But away from their parents and faced with a young, unsure and certainly untrained teacher, student behavior could be a problem. Emery Mulliken remembers a timeless misbehavior: "There was one of the boys who could do things that got the boys near him laughing, but he would appear as though he knew nothing going on." Bradford Smith recollected in an article in the *Proceedings of the Lexington Historical Society V. II* that one teacher lacked control to the point that when he dismissed school, some of the students crawled out the window rather than using the door. Theodore Parker remembers being disciplined for shooting off a popgun at the Smith's End school. Bradford Smith recollected that punishments at the same school depended, of course, on the teacher. One punishment involved holding "a stick at arm's length" and for another the student bent over and put his "finger on the head of a nail on the floor." In both cases the perpetrator had to hold the position for an undetermined amount of time.

Although deterrents differ today, student behavior and teacher responses seem to be timeless. As, it seems, are some elements of a student's school experience.

JULIA STETSON'S SILHOUETTE CIRCA 1830–1835

Silhouettes today appear to be treated as a novelty art form, more often practiced by street artists in tourist areas than by serious practitioners. This was not always so. Before the age of photography, short of commissioning a portrait artist, an expensive proposition then and now, silhouettes offered an affordable alternative when portraying a likeness. Although they do not portray the subject "warts and all," silhouettes do offer a historian some idea of a person's physicality and style.

Etienne de Silhouette, the art form's namesake, served as a finance minister to Louis XV and was so noted for his miserliness that these inexpensive profiles took his name. Later, skilled silhouette cutters such as August Edouart elevated them to an art form. Most popular in the later decades of the eighteenth century and into the nineteenth century, silhouettes fell out of favor with the development of photography. American artists such as the multitalented Charles Wilson Peale practiced the form. Objects as well as people became subjects. William Henry Brown cut a six-foot silhouette of the Dewitt Clinton, one of the first railroad locomotives built in the United States.

A silhouette can be produced in one of three ways. First, a profile could be cut and mounted on background paper. A hollow-cut offers the second option. This involved mounting paper from which the profile was cut instead of the profile itself. Tracing the profile and painting it in a solid color was the third option.

The full-length silhouette, shown here, is that of Mrs. Julia Stetson. Cut and mounted on paper, the identity of the cutter remains unknown, but clues exist. Dean T. Lahikainen, in his book *Lexington Portraits*, notes that Mrs. Stetson's silhouette used the same frame style as Lexington portraits such as those of Eli and Hannah Robbins. Rufus Porter had painted the Robbinses' miniatures. Porter also advertised as a silhouette cutter, but none have ever been credited to him. As an itinerant painter who had produced likenesses of Lexingtonians, Porter clearly spent time in town. The silhouette shows Julia to be slim in physique and middle class in dress. She appears to be no older than middle-aged, probably younger. The style of dress places her from 1830 to 1835, when she was in her late twenties.

Born Julia Ann Merriam, her marriage to Caleb Stetson made her the only one of seven children to marry. She grew up in Buckman Tavern, the youngest daughter of the town's first U.S. postmaster, Rufus Merriam. After marrying Martha Simonds, Merriam had purchased the tavern from his wife's uncle, Joshua Simonds, in 1794. That Merriam must continue the tavern as a public house became a condition of the sale. This he did for more than twenty years. But once Rufus Merriam became postmaster, its days as a public house were numbered. By 1815 it seldom served the public. The southeast wing of the tavern, which he probably added when commissioned in 1813, served as Lexington's post office.

Julia married Caleb Stetson in 1827 when she was twenty-two years old. Stetson had served for three years as principal of Lexington Academy, from 1822 to 1825, after graduating Harvard. He no doubt met Julia while principal at the Academy, since its register reveals that she attended as a student in 1823. The Academy stood a short walk from Buckman Tavern, at the convergence of Hancock Street and Massachusetts Avenue. Lexington Normal School later occupied the same building. Stetson returned to Harvard to attend the Divinity School subsequent to his duties in Lexington. Caleb and Julia married soon after his graduation, ordination and settlement at Medford in 1827. When he retired in 1860, the Stetsons returned to live at Buckman Tavern. Their younger children accompanied them and it is through their daughter Abbie's written recollections that most information on the family survives.

Julia Ann Merriam's marriage made her one of three siblings who left the family homestead. John Parkhurst, the only one who never returned to Buckman Tavern, built a house on Concord Hill, living there alone or with a housekeeper for the rest of his life. Parkhurst's eventual rise through the ranks in the militia led him to be called colonel around town, but family members always called used the familial, Parkis.

Julia's oldest sister Martha's beauty led her to have many suitors, according to family tradition. But she never married, nor did she leave the homestead. The oldest son Rufus slept in the post office wing. Two windows offered a view of an orchard from which the local children would steal fruit. Consequently, Rufus took to shooting from his windows at several targets he set up near the orchard. With the targets showing many hits in the bull's eye, the boys stopped their thievery. Little did they know that he had shot the holes in the target before setting them out.

Emily, next youngest to Julia, suffered blindness as a result of "suppressed measles." She had flown the family nest to become John Parkhurst's housekeeper, but sight failed her. Once housekeeping became impractical, she returned to the family homestead. Emily used ten-pound dumbbells to exercise in her room, sometimes lifting them one thousand times over her head, according to Abbie Stetson's written remembrances. She also exercised by walking back and forth in the garden holding a big blue-green umbrella over her head.

Julia Ann Stetson's silhouette may not bring her to life the way a portrait can. We cannot see the look in her eye or contemplate what she was thinking based on her expression. But the silhouette does place an image in the mind as one contemplates the family interactions at Buckman Tavern in the first half of the nineteenth century.

Lexington

The Ladies of Lexington East village will hold a fair under Canopies in mount Independance on the 14th and various arrangements have been made for the accommodation of visitors. One tent will be fitted up as a Toy shop for children. The Brigade Band is engaged for the occasion There will be an Entertainment at 6 oclock P. M. Tickets for the Entertainment may be had at James Monroe & Co and on the spot. The fair opens at 10 A.M. In case of rain in the morning it will be held on the next day.

The proceeds of this fair are designed to aid in the erection of a Christian Church at East Lexington

Aug 14 1839

There will be a place for refreshments &c &c

DRAFT OF ADVERTISEMENT FOR EAST LEXINGTON FAIR, 1839

Community fairs are a welcome diversion in many New England towns. Any announcement for the East Lexington fair on the Follen Church website boasts of a lineage that reaches deep into the nineteenth century. Whether this tradition has been continuous since 1839 cannot be known for certain. But one expects that many fairs took place in the nineteenth century. The first fair's purpose—to raise funds to build Follen Church, first called the Christian Association—made it the parent of those that followed.

East Village became a vital, growing community in the 1830s with a vibrant fur-dressing industry and gristmill. Eli Robbins owned a fur finishing manufacturing establishment, built by his father Stephen, that employed as many as one hundred people. Also the village's leading benefactor, Eli Robbins built two of the community's important institutions, among other contributions. In 1835, he constructed a great hall, first called Robbins Hall, today the East Lexington Branch Library. He intended this to be a venue for lectures. Indeed, the voices of Emerson, Parker, Sumner and Follen filled the hall not long after. Earlier Robbins had created a three-story observatory on Mount Independence, today the crest of Follen Hill. Some believe that Fern Street is the road he built for travelers to get to the top. Robbins also laid out walks and drives along the perimeter of the summit. As he had planned, this space became a community focal point for recreation. For example, it served early on as the site for annual Fourth of July balls in the village. East Villagers also wanted their own meetinghouse. At a time when distances stretched farther, neighborhood amenities became critical. Not only was making the two-mile trek to the First Parish Unitarian meetinghouse an imposition, but the community had hoped for some degree of autonomy. Previously, in 1833, leading East Villagers, Stephen and Eli Robbins among them, attempted to bring the newly organized Baptist congregation to the village. Later, they had proposed sharing a minister with First Parish in the center. Both attempts failed.

Enter Charles Follen in 1835. Radical political activities led this German émigré to flee his home state of Hesse. Ultimately, he found his way to Harvard College, where he taught his native language. Still a radical, now an abolitionist, he ran afoul of Harvard authorities over his beliefs. Abolitionism at the time was viewed as dangerously divisive and very unpopular. Sought after by several church congregations, Follen came to Lexington to preach his first sermon at Robbins Hall, although one source places his first sermon in the Robbins home. He preached for six months, paid by parishioner contributions. Follen then left to mentor three boys in Watertown for a higher wage. He convinced Ralph Waldo Emerson, then a Unitarian minister, to replace him on a temporary basis. This proved to be Emerson's last ministry. Later Timothy Dwight, as well as several replacement lecturers, followed Emerson.

The Christian Association began raising money to build a meetinghouse in East Village. They had raised $3,200, and prevailed on Follen to return, voicing fear that the Association may break apart without him. With his job as tutor finished, he acceded to their request. Parishioners found a house for him in the village and Follen began to design the new meetinghouse. Its distinguishing feature would be an octagonal floor plan. As a fundraising idea, the women of the Association hit upon sponsoring a fair on Mount Independence. Fairs were a popular fundraising choice in the 1830s. The Robbins women regularly attended the abolitionist fairs that flourished throughout the area.

The document shown here appears to be a draft of a public announcement, perhaps for a Boston newspaper. As such, it reveals interest in reaching an audience beyond Lexington. One of two places where one could purchase advanced tickets was James Munroe's publishing house in Boston. Taking place on August 14 beginning at 10:00 a.m., the advertisement includes a rain date for the fair. It promises that the Brigade Band will entertain and that a tent will be set up as a toyshop for children. The announcement does not indicate a plan for the festivities to extend over several days. Thus, it is not clear whether the decision to continue the fair for three days was ad hoc or planned.

The East Village ladies' met their goal of reaching a wide audience when Boston's *Daily Evening Transcript* wrote a front-page article covering the fair's first day. The article was effusive in its praise for the event, possibly spurring attendance on days two and three. The reporters even rode out to East Lexington on horseback and were first struck by the size of Mount Independence. In a bit of hyperbole, the author wrote that in reality it was a "Mountain whose almost perpendicular sides seemed to defy us." The number of people ascending the "mountain" or enjoying the summit also impressed them. They rode to the top, once assured that it "was practicable." Fancy goods were on sale, its tables manned by "crowds of busy beauties." The organizers used the ground floor of Robbins's large summer home as a rest area, with the porch a popular location to catch a breeze. The author noted that at 6:00 p.m. the leading ladies of the parish gave a "great entertainment," but never specified its nature. Appetites could be sated with "new cheese, brown bread, berries and milk, baked apples" and more. The article ends with the pledge that "no one would be disappointed " if attending the fair the next day. The piece was so thoroughly positive it seems to have been written for the parish's benefit, perhaps the result of a request by a friend.

Mary Swift, at the time a student at Lexington Normal School, traveled to the fair on the first day and recorded her impressions in her journal. From the third floor of the observatory Swift could see the White Mountains and Boston Harbor. The latter she said "appeared like mist over the land." Impressed by the volume of attendees filling the tents, she noted, "groups scattered among the trees." She noted that the refreshment table was "hung with evergreens."

A. Bradford Smith, a child at the time, wrote his recollections of the second day about sixty years later. He remembered that wagons trimmed in evergreen transported the attendees to the summit of Mount Independence. At night there must have been a banquet, since Smith remembers the children having to wait to eat while the adults ate their dinner—a rule that is unimaginable today. Still he thinks he "ate as much as any of them." The observatory was used to sell candles and ice cream. Later that night Francis Bowman led an auction that raised about $1,200.

East Lexington's fair today is established as an annual fall event. That the organizers today give tribute to those who organized the first is testimony to their respect for the event's history.

First Normal School House Belfast opened July, 1834.

View of Normal School House near Lexington

PENCIL SKETCH OF NORMAL SCHOOL, CIRCA 1840

Correcting the shortcomings of the public schools, an ongoing issue today, also occupied the public discourse early in the nation's history. Even as the nation finished its first fifty years, dissatisfaction over public education began to take root—particularly in Massachusetts. In 1827 the state ordered towns to send statistics regarding its schools to the Secretary of the Commonwealth. The data confirmed what most knew: the district schools, rather than improving, were actually declining. Leaders in Massachusetts made the education of teachers central to school reform. Fittingly, Lexington became home to the nation's first public teacher training institution in 1839. A Normal School student drew the sketch of the building, shown here.

Massachusetts began its reforms by establishing a Board of Education in 1837—the first in the nation. Horace Mann became the first secretary of the Board of Education, holding the position for twelve years. About the same time, wealthy Boston merchant Edmund Dwight offered to contribute $10,000 toward improving educational facilities in the state. The Board decided to use this as seed money to fund schools to train teachers. The host town would be responsible for supplying the building and some of the operating expenses. The state planned two such schools—one each in the eastern and western part of the state. Lexington competed with several towns to host the first normal school in the east. When it opened, Lexington Normal School became the first and only one operating for several years.

That an unused school building already stood in Lexington made it an attractive choice as a host town. Originally, the building now standing at the junction of Bedford and Hancock Streets was constructed in 1823 to house the Lexington Academy, a private college preparatory school. After the Academy's closing, the Lexington Manual Seminary used the facilities in 1833, but only for a short time.

For many citizens, private schools such as the Lexington Academy symbolized the problem with public education. Because of inadequate district school education, parents with means sent their children to private academies. This two-tiered system led many to worry about future of equality and democracy in the new nation. This issue of fairness in educational opportunity resonates still today. Horace Mann's goal was public schools "open to the poorest; good enough for the richest."

American interest in the teacher training sprung from dissatisfaction with district schools instruction. By and large, young men working their way through college taught the winter term. The meager pay (in Lexington twenty-eight dollars for the term) and their lack of long-term commitment to teaching led to many ineffective teachers who were simply passing through. Mann estimated that of six thousand teachers in district schools in Massachusetts, barely two hundred of them considered it a life profession.

Early in the century young women taught the summer term usually to the youngest children because their older siblings worked in season on the farm. Towns paid these women even less. Furthermore, these teenaged teachers possessed no more than a district school education themselves. The normal school experiment coincided with several forces that led the public schools' teachers to be increasingly female. In addition to the lower cost, the West and new industries had begun to attract men from the teaching ranks. This happened at a time when a growing number of schools increased demand for teachers. Finally, the idealized image of women at the time was as moral exemplars. Who better to teach the young?

The normal school curriculum sought to impart pedagogical technique, as well as the content knowledge students should have. American normal schools patterned themselves after teacher training institutions in Prussia and France. At the time Prussian village schools were generally acknowledged as the finest in the world. Their teachers were trained as professionals to pursue teaching as a career. "Normal school" comes from the name for French teacher training schools, école normale.

Aware of the symbolism, Horace Mann wanted the first Lexington Normal School term to begin on April 19, 1839. But the school's opening was delayed. The first three students arrived on July 3, 1839, and were admitted after passing an entrance exam. Before additional students began arriving, these three must have wondered if they made the right choice in traveling from their homes in Lincoln, West Cambridge (Arlington) and Charlestown for this venture. Unitarian minister Cyrus Pierce, the school's first principal and its only teacher, privately harbored similar concerns over the fate of the normal experiment. Within several days a few more students arrived. By September twelve students made up the class. More would follow. During its Lexington years thirty-eight young ladies made up the Normal School's largest class.

Cyrus Pierce kept a journal into which he poured his reactions to the day's work. He could be hard on himself as well as his students, although he rarely voiced his unhappiness to them. A variety of activities filled his day. He lectured to his students on pedagogy. His Normal School students kept journals that Pierce read and appraised, a method used today. He set up a model school, in which they could practice, with students taking turns serving as principal each month. Presumably, the thirty-six ten-year-old boys and girls were Lexington children. Pierce observed his teachers' practice, then provided feedback. He taught model lessons. In his words he tried to impart the "art of teaching" and the "science of school government." He opposed the emphasis on rote memorization, the prevailing method of the day. None of his teachers, Pierce wrote of the teaching of grammar, would require "pupils to commit the whole textbook to memory, before looking at the nature of words and their application in the structure of sentences." He also warned against humiliating students.

By "government" Pierce meant classroom management. Shortcomings in this area presented a serious problem to the district school. In 1837 400 out of 2,800 winter terms ended because "big boys" effectively chased the often younger and physically smaller teacher out of school. Pierce preached to his students "that the secret of good order is in your breast—and you must bring it out." He taught that a commanding presence and manner went a long way toward earning respect.

Mary Swift, a Quaker from Nantucket and his star pupil, also kept a journal. While Pierce's journal focuses strictly on the Normal School, Swift records activities on days off. This meant that she recorded her forays into Lexington. Every Sunday she attended the meetinghouse on the Common "all day," along with several other churches. She also accompanied Pierce to the first East Lexington Fair on Mount Independence. Swift and fifteen of her classmates took the stagecoach to East Village to attend the dedication of its new church in 1840. She dined at Benjamin Muzzey's mansion house. Clearly, the girls became a presence in the everyday life of Lexington.

Lexington Normal School welcomed a constant stream of visitors. Notables such as Bronson Alcott and Samuel Gridley Howe wanted to observe this experiment. Howe later hired Mary Swift to help him with his work with the blind. Among the local visitors were Benjamin Muzzey,

Benjamin Wellington and Charles Tidd. Lexington did financially support the school, but as this became more of a hardship, the school moved. Samuel J. May had taken over as principal for the final two years after Pierce resigned due to failing health. In 1844 the school moved to West Newton, then to Framingham in 1854, where it became the first of the Massachusetts normal school system, later to be called teacher colleges.

Beginning in 1851 the alumna held yearly reunions at the Lexington House. Many had gone on to teach and remembered fondly their pioneering work. Principal Cyrus Pierce wrote in 1851, at a Normal School reunion, that the participants waged "the battle against ignorance and bad teaching on the plains of Lexington, already renowned in history for another and far different conflict."

LEXINGTON HOUSE,

LEXINGTON.
GORHAM BIGELOW, PROPRIETOR.

BILL OF FARE.

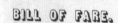

AT THE LEXINGTON HOUSE,
JANUARY 14, 1852.

ROAST.

Turkey, Mongrel Geese, Capron, Chickens,

ENTREES.

Escolloped Oysters,   Oysters Stewed.
Chicken Sallad,   Lobster Sallad.

GAME.

Canvas Back Ducks,   Grouse,   Wigeon,
Black Ducks,   Quails,   Partridges.

PASTRY.

Charlotte Ruse,   Pies,   Tarts,   Custards,
Italian Cream,   Jellies,   Ice Cream.

DESSERT.

Apples,   Pears,   Oranges,   Grapes,   Dry Fruit,
TEA AND COFFEE. *Chocolate*

GORHAM BIGELOW, PROPRIETOR.

C. Rand's Press, Charlestown.

LEXINGTON HOUSE ADVERTISING CARD AND BILL OF FARE 1852

Hotel options in Lexington have been slim for quite some time for a variety of reasons. The Battle Green Inn remains the only choice for the traveler who wants to stay in the business district. In the nineteenth century several large and successful hotels prospered near the center of town. The heyday of Lexington's hotel era really began after the Civil War, when the railroad's full effect of affording easy access to Boston combined with increased urbanization. Large hotels such as Massachusetts House and Russell House attracted travelers who liked to "summer" in town as well as those planning winter sleighing parties. But Lexington's transition from tavern to hotel began even before the Civil War. One hotel was built to coincide with the town's entrance into the railroad era in 1846. It came to be named Lexington House.

In 1846 tavern owner Benjamin Muzzey became the mastermind behind Lexington's participation in a railroad network—the Lexington and West Cambridge Railroad. Muzzey owned the Monument House, situated on the site of today's CVS on Massachusetts Avenue. Concerned that transportation advances in the form of turnpikes and canals shifted traffic away from the center, Muzzey worked to secure a railroad running through the town center. In anticipation of an increase in travelers seeking overnight accommodations, he tore down Monument House in 1847 and built a new much larger public house in its place at the cost of $20,000— finished only months after railroad service began. The new center depot delivered travelers within easy walking distance to this expansive, elegant building he called Muzzey's Hotel.

About 150 years ago a three-story house with two extended wings, fronted by large porches, stood at the intersection of Waltham and Massachusetts Avenue. Resting on top sat a cupola. Unfortunately, Muzzey died the same year it opened. His railroad never became a financial success for investors, but it had substantial influence on Lexington's development. At some point renamed Lexington House, his hotel passed through a succession of owners with Gorham Bigelow during the 1850s being the most popular. Bigelow had earlier run a tavern in City Square in Boston in 1835. His advertising card shown here (top) depicts a bucolic scene, one difficult for the modern-day viewer to imagine in the center of the business district. The hotel did a brisk business for a time. Charles Hudson, in the first edition of *History of Lexington*, wrote that it "was well filled with boarders." With easy access to Boston, perhaps a few chose to live in Lexington and commute to the city—a phenomenon more common later in the century. The advertising card shows the hotel standing at the center of activity with people arriving by stage and chaise, but not those stepping off the train in the rear.

Lexington House did not simply provide overnight accommodations for boarders and travelers, however. Just as taverns were integral to Lexington social life, so was Lexington House. Extant advertisements and brochures reveal the hotel as an important gathering place for community events, including vocal and instrumental concerts, musicals, exhibitions, celebrations and reunions. In short, the hotel became the premier public space in town due to its capacity and central location. The town hall built on the site of Muzzey apartments the same year as Lexington House hosted some events, but it was limited in size. Certainly, some taverns such as Cutler's in East Lexington remained a popular venue for dances. Many events at Lexington House seemed to center on higher cultural pursuits than some dances and balls, perhaps attracting a particular type of audience.

Lexington seemed also to be a place to enjoy an elegant meal. The advertising card shown here (bottom) offers a menu for supper dated January 14, 1852. The bill of fare boasts options for a sumptuous meal. Around mid-century, American eating patterns began to change in some ways. Dinner, the noon meal, traditionally had been the main one. An early evening supper offered light eating; some people skipped it entirely. But as the workplace moved further from the household, men found returning home for a large meal difficult. Consequently, the large meal began to be reserved for early evening hour after the workday ended. The meals in these early hotels tended not to be served at the diner's pleasure. Rather, set times for each meal were posted. Although not specified on this menu, one published a year later by the same proprietor, Gorham Bigelow, listed breakfast at 6:15 a.m., tea at 1:00 p.m. and supper at 7:00 p.m. Presumably, anyone arriving at 8:00 p.m. expecting to dine was out of luck.

At some point Lexington House no longer made a profit for the owner, or perhaps Gorham Bigelow wanted to get out of the business or retire. The onset of the Civil War certainly took its toll on the railroad and probably affected hotel trade also. Dio Lewis, a physician and educator, purchased the building in 1864 to host a boarding school for girls. Hudson writes that Lewis greatly improved the grounds and buildings, implying that they had begun to show age and disrepair. Lewis's interest was in showing how physical exercise aided in promoting health and learning. Consequently, he particularly encouraged parents of daughters in delicate health to enroll in his school. Come they did from all over the country, as well as several from outside the United States. Unfortunately, a fire destroyed the building that began as Muzzey's Hotel in 1867 and Lewis never returned. The site became the location of the new town hall, built in 1871.

Most Lexingtonians who walk the ground in and around CVS remain unaware that if they were transported back in time 150 years, they would be standing in an elegant hotel. It is unlikely that, given today's traffic patterns, the town will see its like.

April 28, '60

Voted to elect the following officers for the ensuing year
    E. R. Bullard   Presedent
    M. B. Smith   Vice President
    G. H. Lawrence.   Sec. Treas.
Voted that the Sec. be Ex-officio
Voted that the name of this club be called "Zephyr"

Voted to except of this constitution

Voted to play the Massachusetts game of Base Ball

Voted to reconsider the vote whereby we voted to play
the Massachusetts game of Base. Ball

May 7th

    Voted play once a week on Saturaday at 6 o'clk.
    Voted to fine each member 12 cts if not onduty
when called for

    Voted to buy two bats & balls

    Voted to have one spare bat

    Voted to have a lock & key on the Hall door

    Voted to fine each member 25 cts if leaves the game
without the consent of the Commanding Officer

    Voted to have the bat & Ball left at the hall

May 12th

    Voted to reconsider the vote whereby we voted to have
a squeare Bat

    Voted to have a reccord book

EAST LEXINGTON ZEPHYRS BASE BALL CLUB MINUTES OF MEETING, 1860

The emotions on display during a Red Sox–Yankees series make it difficult to conceive of a time when baseball did not place competition above all else. But this was the case for many baseball clubs in the 1850s and 1860s, including the East Lexington Zephyr Base Ball club. The minutes of their meetings and the club's constitution are all that remain to trace their activities.

Warren Goldstein writes in *Playing for Keeps*, "In the late 1850s, baseball was a club-based fraternal pastime." First and foremost, the Zephyrs was a club, with members paying one dollar in membership dues. The baseball club's president was E.R. Bullard, with M.B. Smith the vice-president and G.H. Lawrence secretary-treasurer. Formed in April 24, 1860, the club's "Rules and Regulations" deal exclusively with its governance. The constitution makes no mention of baseball. It lists the titles of the officers, their responsibilities, their terms and the election process, as well as the frequency and conduct of meetings. Minutes of the meetings, however, do deal with baseball matters—just not actual games. The club made some important decisions in its first meeting on April 18, the minutes of which are shown here. The Zephyrs voted to play the Massachusetts game, but later in the meeting voted to reconsider. Subsequent minutes do not reveal their eventual choice. This was a critical decision since this determined the rules, the playing field, the number of players and, therefore, the tenor of their play. The other choice was to play according to the New York rules. Tom Kelleher has calculated that fifty-nine New England teams were playing Massachusetts baseball by 1858, while eighteen Massachusetts teams had begun playing by New York rules. The latter would prove to be the wave of the future.

Although different versions of the Massachusetts rules existed within New England previously, the Massachusetts Association of Baseball Players codified the rules in 1858. The Massachusetts game, once called town ball, had evolved from the earlier game of rounders. Rather than canvas bags, stakes were arrayed in a square sixty feet apart to serve as the four bases. Twelve to fourteen team members played the field without set positions. Since there was no foul territory, any ball hit was in play. Consequently, some batters hit the ball behind them, causing injury to the catcher as a strategy. With no foul territory, only one out ended an inning. Anything hit could be caught for an out, but fly balls had to be caught in the air. Also, "soaking," or hitting a base runner with a thrown ball, could achieve an out. One rule made for extremely long games—it ended only when one team scored one hundred runs. Except for the fly ball rule, these rules bore little resemblance to the modern game.

The Knickerbockers Base Ball Club in New York City codified the New York game. Like the modern game, they played on a diamond with canvas bags ninety feet apart. In 1848 they began allowing the tag of a base as an out rather than "soaking" the runner. Nine players per team played set positions and batted in an established order. Only a ball hit between first and third was in play. By 1857 a team won by having the highest score after nine innings. Also, three outs made up an inning. These rules led to a faster game without the danger caused by throwing the ball at the runner or hitting the ball backward at the catcher. Baseball historians today credit the Knickerbockers with inventing the modern game.

Both the Massachusetts and New York rules required a round bat, although the former specified the bat be covered in leather. Gloves were not in use then. The Zephyrs decided to store the equipment under lock and key at the "Hall." Where was the hall? Was it Village Hall? The Universalist Church had been using Village Hall, but it closed in 1859 so that is possible. Another possibility was Cutler's Tavern. Albert Byrant writes that a large hall was added to the tavern. Warren Goldstein notes that it was customary for "club rooms" to be in a hotel or tavern. Edwin Worthen remembers baseball being played by the railroad tracks in East Village when he was a child in the 1890s. But baseball fields usually endure, if not built upon. This would have placed the field near Cutler Tavern, where Arlex Oil stands today.

The Zephyrs also voted to play once a week on Saturdays at six o'clock. Later in July they increased the frequency to Tuesdays, Thursdays and Saturdays. Attendance problems seem to have recurred, since the club voted to fine members not "on duty" for a game. As many as twelve members belonged to the club, but they "discharged" two members in the ensuing months, perhaps over attendance issues. On May 12 the club voted to "have the bat and ball remain in the hall unless there be five or more members to play."

The minutes never even hint at competition with another team. It was not unusual for a club such as this to play only "practice games" among themselves. On the other hand, spirited competition between teams and participation in leagues also were firmly established norms by then. In June 1857 the Boston Olympics played the Wassapoag team of Sharon, Massachusetts, in the final game of a best of three series in front of two thousand spectators. In 1860 thirty teams played in the Boston vicinity. If the Zephyrs did play another team, the traditional prize would have been the game ball, to be kept in their clubroom. After the game the home team would host a dinner at a local tavern. Cutlers would have been the appropriate venue for the Zephyrs.

The minutes end October 25, 1860, with the discharge of C.W. Sullivan. While the journal exists today as disconnected pages, the final entry ends in the middle of the page. Perhaps this indicates that the club lasted about seven months. Certainly, baseball season was at its end. Events were about to take over some members' lives soon. A week later the election of Abraham Lincoln would be followed by South Carolina's secession from the Union. In December of the following year, the Zephyr President E.R. Bullard would die in the Civil War. Club member Ralph Cole also served in the Union army for two years. Many soldiers brought their baseball bats with them. The Civil War is credited with spreading the game of baseball geographically, expanding rapidly in the Northeast and Midwest in the postwar years.

att a meeting of ye Freehol[ders]
Town of Lexington Duly [met]
may: 19: 1755: Did then take [in]
Choyce of Mr. Jonas Clarke for [ ]
Did so far Concur with ye Ch[urch]
& ye Nays were: 16: then ye [ ]
for Mr. Clarke in Case he se[ ]
half of ye Sum to be paid 6 [ ]
moyety 18 months after his [ ]
to be his yearly Sallery for [ye]
minestrey in this town: als[o]
takes up & is Settled as our [ ]
Quit all manner of Claim t[o ye]
part of ye Minesterial Lan[d]
Chose a Committee to wait o[n]
vvz: Dea: Brown Dea: Ston[e]
Capt: Saml: Stone. Mr. Robt: [ ]
James Brown: & also to Desi[re]
ye: 14th Day of July next t[o ye]
ajourned & also to Suppl[y]

MATTERS OF FINANCE

Boston June 9: 1743

Recd of Mr Isaac Stone One Hundred
Pounds old Tenour in full for a Negroe
Woman called Betty sold him &c

£100:0:0

Pr John Avery

817

ISAAC STONE PURCHASES A SLAVE, 1743

Northerners today take satisfaction in the knowledge that on the eve of the Civil War, their ancestors likely stood on the right side of the slavery issue. Since slavery existed legally only below the Mason Dixon line at that time, Southerners referred to human bondage as their "peculiar institution." In the years before the Revolutionary War, however, slavery was not particular only to the South. It existed throughout the thirteen colonies to varying degrees and in different forms. Massachusetts in 1641 actually became the first colony to make slavery legal. As this bill of sale for the purchase of a slave named Betty indicates, Lexington was no exception.

People of prominence, those most likely to have papers to preserve, find their way into recorded history easily. Reconstructing the lives of ordinary folk in the seventeenth and eighteenth centuries, however, poses problems due to lack of manuscript sources. Tracing the lives of slaves presents even more difficulty, as the historian must rely on indirect sources. Whites authored most of the available evidence, sometimes in their letters or journals, but more often in the form of legal and administrative transactions such as probate records, bills of sale or in the vital records of towns.

This bill of sale documents a transaction made in Boston during which Isaac Stone of Lexington purchased a female slave for one hundred pounds on June 9, 1743. Where did one go in Boston to purchase a slave? If Stone purchased Betty at a slave auction, its location could have been anywhere in the city. Boston set aside no special place for such auctions. Merchants used their stores or the warehouses holding the slaves. Dealers who owned taverns might use these as a venue for auctioning slaves.

Isaac Stone paid one hundred pounds in "old tenour." This refers to an early run of paper money that had devalued by 1743. By that time, two other emissions of paper money called new tenor and middle tenor were also in circulation. Therefore, the purchase price of one hundred pounds, quite high depending on Betty's age, is deceptive today. Betty does not appear in Lexington vital records or Charles Hudson's genealogies. Her stay in Lexington might have been short, as it does not appear that she married, gave birth or died in town.

Born in Lexington around 1695, Stone was about forty-eight at the time of purchase. Stone appears never to have married so he probably bought Betty for domestic work. A man of prominence, in four years he would be elected selectman. A slaveholder in Lexington had to be a person of means given the price of slaves. Later, Stone donated a bell for public use in 1761, inspiring the town to build the belfry to enclose it.

According to valuations, Lexington appeared to average about twenty slaves for much of the eighteenth century. In 1754, the Massachusetts General Court ordered towns to take a slave census. Lexington recorded twenty-four. Charles Hudson writes that by 1775 the number had shrunk to five. What might their lives have been like? Probably most Lexington slave owners had no more than one or two slaves. Benjamin Muzzey's probate inventory in 1732 lists "1 Negro man and a Negro woman and child." Francis Bowman's 1744 will left three slaves named Ballis, Phillis and Pompey. Most likely, these constituted the largest slaveholdings in Lexington at the time. Without large plantations producing staple crops, no need existed for gang labor with separate living quarters. It is likely males worked on the farm doing similar tasks as their masters and women performed household chores.

With a high white to black ratio, the constant interaction with the owner's family meant assimilation into white culture happened more fully. African culture, therefore, while certainly surviving in some forms, persisted more subtly in towns such as Lexington than in towns of South Carolina. The opportunity for African culture to be reinforced and passed on could not compare with a plantation's slave quarters. In New England, slaves lived as subordinate members of white households. The slave usually ate with the family in small farmhouses. In part, this is simply a practical accommodation to sparse slave populations, but it also reflects the different approach toward slavery that New England took.

Make no mistake—slaves were considered property, listed in probate records along with the livestock. They could be sold away from family members. Betty had no choice in her sale; she may have left loved ones behind. White reference to slaves in the records often leaves no doubt as to their status. Betty was a "negro women [sic] called Betty," as if her name was not integral to her identity. Town records often referred to slaves as "Brown's Negro" with reference to the owner only. This presents further difficulty in tracing slave life.

Nonetheless, under Massachusetts law and tradition slaves fell somewhere between a plantation slave and an indentured servant. Rooted in its Puritan past, this approach to involuntary servitude followed the Jewish model. The slave was, in some ways, a member of the owner's family and in the Hebraic tradition referred to as a servant. Hence, they became both persons and property. In contrast to the South, for example, slave marriages were legally recognized.

As might be expected, owners encouraged slaves to convert to Christianity. Many became members of the Congregational church. Since status determined the seating in Congregational churches, slaves sat together in a segregated area. In Lexington, the meetinghouse relegated its slaves to the balcony. Some church burial grounds had special areas set aside for slave parishioners. There seems to be no headstone representing an African American in Lexington's First Parish burial grounds. The First Parish records do show a number of African American members. "Robert _____, a Negro" in 1739 and "Lucy Sawco, a Negro servant to Mr. Robert Harrington" in 1757 were baptized and admitted to the church. Some made deathbed conversions. Pomp Blackman, a Revolutionary war veteran, no longer a slave and clearly on his deathbed, was baptized and admitted the day before he died.

Alice Hinkle in *Prince Estabrook, Slave and Soldier*, calculates that nine African Americans served as part of Lexington's quota in the Revolutionary War, most connected to the town. These included slaves such as Prince Estabrook and Pompey Blackman, both probably earning their freedom as a result. Also among the nine were Silas and Eli Burdoo, most likely free people of color.

The rhetoric of freedom invoked throughout the Revolutionary era seemed incompatible with slavery. With war still raging, Massachusetts adopted its state constitution in 1780. In 1783, the Massachusetts Supreme Judicial Court pronounced, in freeing Quock Walker, that slavery violated the rights granted in the Massachusetts Constitution. The first state to legalize slavery became the first to abolish it.

At a meeting of ye Freeholder & other Inhabitants of y^e
Town of Lexington Duly warned & orderly assembled on
may: 19: 1755: Did then take into Consideration ye Churches
Choyce of Mr Jonas Clarke for their Pastor & ye Congreegation
Did So far Concur with s^d Choyce as ye thay brought in: 51: yeas
& ye Nays were: 16: then ye town voted: 133-6-8 Settlement
for Mr Clarke in Case he Settles with us as our Pastor ye one
half of s^d Sum to be paid 6 months after his ordination ye other
moyety 18 months after his Ordination: also voted: 80 pounds
to be his yearly Sallery for to Support him in ye work of y^e
minestrey in this town: also voted ye s^d Mr Clarke in Case he
takes up & is Settled as our Pastor Shall as Shuch forever
Quit all manner of Claim title or Intrest in or unto aney
part of ye Minesterial Land in this town: then ye town
Chose a Committee to wait on Mr Clarke with ye above s votes
vvz: Dea: Brown Dea: Stone Isaac Bowsman Will Reed Esqr
Capt Sam^{ll} Stone. Mr Robt Harrington Josiah Parker & M^r
James Brown: & also to Desire Mr Clarks answer at or before
ye 14th Day of July next to which Day this meeting Stands
ajourned & also to Supply our Pulpit ye mean time

A true Copey attest Josiah Parker Town Clerk

THE MINISTER'S SETTLEMENT
1755

Political issues have divided Lexington recently, replicating, to a degree, the cultural divide that exists nationally. Colonial towns were no less susceptible to division over controversial issues. No concern threatened the harmony of a New England town more than the selection of its minister. Following the customary practice of a vote of the membership, two camps could quickly form among those who favored a choice and the dissenters. This could leave a residual tension that may linger for years. Such was the case in Salem, and it contributed to the Salem witchcraft hysteria. Concord also divided over religious issues, and it contributed to political divisions in the Revolutionary War. Such was not the case in Lexington, when it sought a successor for John Hancock, who served from 1697–1752. Instead, the eventual choice of Jonas Clarke led to another extended period of community harmony. His settlement, or contract, is shown here. It marked the beginning of Clarke's fifty-year ministry. No doubt many residents at the time of his selection would have been satisfied if he could just approach the accomplishments of his predecessor.

Hancock's fifty-five year tenure in Lexington was responsible in large measure for this smooth transition. (Note: He was the grandfather of the more famous Patriot leader and governor John Hancock.) His forceful personality, scholarship and wisdom led to esteem not limited to his Lexington congregation. For his last thirty years, Hancock became the senior minister in Middlesex County, chairing ordination councils for twenty-one local ministers. As a mark of respect, he was often called "the Bishop." Known as a peacemaker, Hancock possessed no small measure of practical good sense. This quality served him well during the 1740s when controversial doctrinal issues divided towns such as Concord and Salem.

Briefly, this controversy pitted New Light, or evangelical ministers, such as Northampton minister Jonathan Edwards, against Old Light or traditional ministers. New Light advocates criticized Old Light ministers as staid and too rational, having drifted from the strict Calvinism that had brought their ancestors to New England. For New Light ministers, conversions or born again experiences were more critical requirements for the ministry than an education at Harvard or Yale. The heart took precedence over the mind. They feared Old Light ministers were drifting from Calvinist beliefs of human depravity, election and predestination. Some liberal or Arminian ministers even showed signs of believing in free will. New Light ministers led emotional, very entertaining revivals, gathering numerous converts, often splitting established churches in the process.

Hancock wisely took a middle ground during this period. He believed himself to be an orthodox Calvinist, who never abandoned the sect's core beliefs, but he valued rational thought. Although he objected to the extremes of the Great Awakening, he did so quietly. Nor did he denounce Arminians. As a result of this politically pragmatic approach, he actually added eighty new members to his church in 1741 and 1742. When Hancock died on December 6, 1752, at eighty-one, it was truly the end of an era. Fittingly, the modest Lexington farmers held an elaborate funeral for Hancock that cost 200 pounds. Little did Lexington residents realize that a new era would soon begin.

The town quickly chose a committee to supply the pulpit until a decision could be made on a settled or permanent minister. Substitute pastors lectured for a few Sundays each. This also served also as an audition for the congregation to take the measure of the minister's work, if he decided to apply for settlement. On April 8, 1754, Lexington town meeting voted to "keep a day of fasting and prayer on the 25th of the above said April in preparation for said choice." In June it extended an invitation to Mr. Aaron Putnam. He turned it down because the vote to invite him fell short of unanimity. Perhaps Putnam feared a division in the congregation that might hamper his ministry at the outset. Consequently, several other ministers "auditioned," Jonas Clarke among them. He had graduated Harvard College in the same year Hancock died. In May of 1755 the congregation voted to invite Jonas Clarke to be its permanent pastor. As the document notes, the vote also fell short of unanimity, fifty-one to sixteen. Clarke did not see this as an impediment to his success.

Then the "freeholders and other inhabitants" voted the settlement. Were they not members of the congregation? Almost without exception they attended the same services, but official church membership had standards not all achieved. They were taxpayers, however, and should have a say in the allocation of revenue. The terms of the settlement was 133 pounds, six shillings and eight pence, one half to be paid six months after he was ordained, the rest one year after that. After that Clarke would be paid a yearly salary of 80 pounds. The town attached a caveat prohibiting the new minister from any claim to the ministerial lands, a stretch of land purchased by inhabitants of Cambridge Farms parish to provide for the settling of ministers. It composed the Parker Street playing fields from Worthen Road to Waltham Street.

The offer to settle a minister often began a contract negotiation. Clarke seemed concerned that the sacrifice of claim to the ministerial lands would leave him short of wood, a critical commodity in New England. So he negotiated an amendment to the settlement—that the town would supply twenty cords of wood yearly beginning three years after ordination. A yearly wood supply was actually a common part of a minister's settlement.

Jonas Clarke lived in the parsonage, now called the Hancock-Clarke House, still standing today on Hancock Street. This included a fifty-acre farm that extended toward the Common, including the land the Masonic Building now occupies. Mrs. Hancock still lived there when Clarke arrived, however. So the bachelor Reverend Clarke boarded with her. There he met Lucy Bowes, Hancock's granddaughter, who began living with her grandmother. In 1754 her father, Reverend Nicholas Bowes of Bedford, had decided to serve as chaplain in the army during the French and Indian War. Earlier, Bowes surrendered his pulpit over what seemed to be a doctrinal dispute. In 1757 Clarke married Lucy Bowes, becoming a Hancock by marriage. His service to Lexington matched Hancock's in length, 1755–1805, and quality.

Clarke's personality was strong, but like Hancock, he stayed away from theological controversies. Clarke remained within the tolerant Calvinist tradition of his predecessor, thus achieving a harmony by welcoming a wide range of religious opinions. But it was Clarke's political influence that earned his place in the nation's history. As troubles with England increased for the colonies, Clarke emerged as the undisputed town political leader. He did, of course, have a family connection to the cause. Merchant and Patriot John Hancock was Lucy Bowes's cousin. In fact, Hancock had lived in the parsonage with his grandfather during some of his childhood years. But family connection aside, Clarke's beliefs motivated his political position. His library and writing reflect someone grounded in Whig ideology. Clarke wrote almost every town resolve and instruction to Lexington representatives from the Stamp Act crisis through the Washington administration. He was

Lexington's contact for Patriot leaders. Of course, Revere headed straight to Clarke's parsonage the night of April 18, 1775, to warn his guests, John Hancock and Sam Adams, of the British approach.

Clarke's personality and political leadership, as well as the theological harmony he and Reverend John Hancock had inculcated, contributed to Lexington's virtual unanimity in adopting the Patriot cause. For over one hundred years the town could not have been in better hands.

Advertisement.

STray'd or stolen out of the Pasture of the Subscriber, the Night of the 4th Instant, a large Horse near fifteen Hands high, Chesnut colour'd, with a large Blaze in his Face, with some white Hairs in his Mein and Tail, trots and paces both, and is six Years old.

Whoever shall take up said Horse, and return him to the Owner, or give certain Intelligence so that the Owner may recover said Horse again, shall have Four Dollars Reward, and all necessary Charges paid, by me

WILLIAM REED.

Lexington, *July* 6. 1775.

WILLIAM REED'S HANDBILL
FOR A LOST HORSE, 1775

Imagine a Lexington landscape in which horses and cows wander from the pasture and where hogs roam the land, occasionally rooting in vegetable gardens. This was Lexington in the eighteenth century. The town assessors in 1748 reported 236 oxen, 598 cows, 147 horses, 746 sheep and 240 hogs within its boundaries—close to three times the number of people. For this farming community, livestock was integral to its economy. Although the town routinely allowed hogs to roam free, farmers sought the return of their other animals.

When these animals strayed, the owner had two options. One appears here. Dated July 6, 1775, this advertisement offers a reward for the return of a large horse or for information leading to it. That the owner allowed for the possibility of its having been stolen reveals horse thievery to be at least a sporadic occurrence. It also explains the reward for information. The owner, William Reed, is likely to have posted it in a prominent place such as Buckman Tavern. Centrally located and regularly frequented, it was also the focal point of "nooning" on Sabbath days at the time. Many congregants spent the lunchtime break between morning and afternoon lecture in or around Buckman.

For the twenty-first-century reader, the text of the advertisement can be difficult to read because the typographic long "s" looks like an "f." Yet closer inspection reveals that it differs from the "f" by having a minimal cross-stroke. As with any advertisement today for a stray cat or dog, a physical description accompanies it. Unlike today, no way to contact Reed appears. The limited town population and the prominence of the family precluded the necessity.

The William Reed referred to may be one of three generations living in Lexington then. The eldest, age eighty-three at the time, was the son of one of the original settlers in Cambridge Farms. In the early 1700s, he was captain of a militia company that explored the frontier in response to the town's fear of Indian attack. Like his father, Reed became a selectman and represented Lexington in the Massachusetts General Court. The use of "esquire" often attached to his name in the records also indicates his stature. The Reed farm lay on the north side of town, bounded by Cedar Street, Katahdin Woods, Hartwell Avenue, Garfield Street and the Minuteman Bikeway. In 1737, the farm housed fifty sheep, fourteen cows and six oxen. By 1775, it obviously acquired at least one horse. Due to the elder Reed's age, the author of the ad probably was his fifty-six-year-old son. Another possibility was his grandson, also named William. Since he was part of Captain Parker's militia company on April 19 and later in Cambridge, he may have not been in Lexington at the time.

Due to their importance to the economy and their potential for nuisance, the regulation of stray animals was a town government imperative. Checking the town pound, which served as a holding area for stray livestock, was Reed's second option. Most likely, its absence from the pound prompted the advertisement. If it appeared there later, Reed would pay a fine, rather than a reward. Immediately upon Lexington's incorporation in 1713, the selectmen directed Benjamin Wellington to build a pound to be about thirty feet square with five rails. Michael Canavan wrote in 1900 that the pound had stood on the location of the present Hancock Church. It often had "inmates." The town records show that on November 1, 1718, alone a "chestnut mare," "brown steer," "black mare" and "red steer" were impounded. Also, sheep often found their way into the pound. In 1713, town meeting voted Lieutenant John Munroe the first "keeper of the pound." He and his sons served in that capacity sporadically for many years. Since he and later his son Marrett owned a house, now 905 Massachusetts Avenue, near the pound, the town made a logical choice. This branch of the Munroe family owned one hundred acres on that side of the Common, bounded by Massachusetts Avenue, Clarke Street, Hill Street and Concord Hill. Three days before Reed's advertisement Marrett Munroe became the town pound keeper.

Among the livestock that received special attention were hogs. Town meeting voted routinely to allow "swine to goe at large" as long as their owners yoked and marked them with rings. The hog reeve, also elected by town meeting, assumed the responsibility for assuring they were marked with a ring and yoke. A ring in the snout prevented the animal from rooting, and the yoke, of specified dimensions, secured gardens and other enclosures from mischievous intrusion. On occasion, they trespassed in gardens. If the hog reeve discovered an unmarked hog or one foraging in someone's garden, he deposited it in the town pound and fined the owner. Awarding the position of hog reeve to recent newlyweds was a tradition in New England towns, probably with roots in England. In 1713 the town appointed six men as hog reeves, Nathaniel Bunktline, John Muzzey, Jonathan Robinson, James Russell, Josiah Hubs Jr. and John Cooper. By 1773, the number of hog reeves had reduced to three but were augmented by two deer reeves. These were responsible for controlling the hunting of increasingly scarce deer.

No record exists of Reed finding his wayward mare. Since it is dated just two days after the horse disappeared, one can hope it found its way back home. In that case, it would have cost Reed no money.

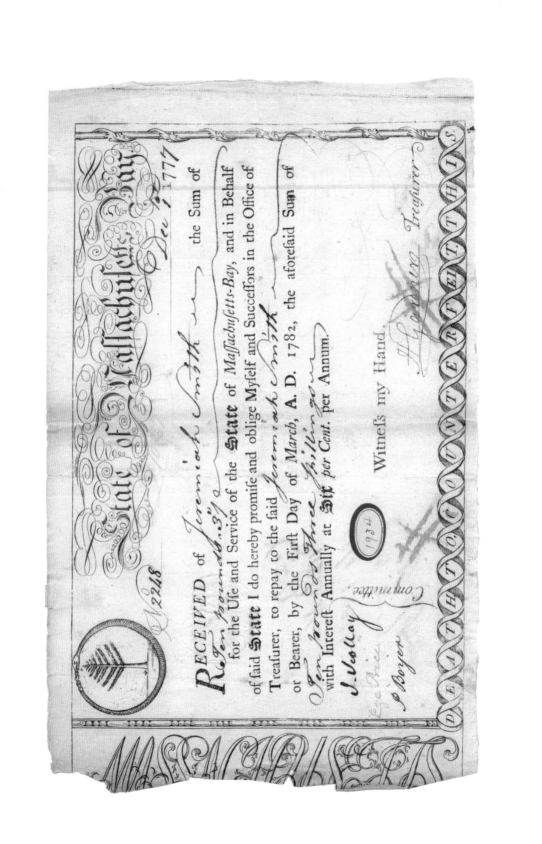

No. 2248

State of Massachusetts Bay

Dec 7 1777

RECEIVED of Jeremiah Smith ⸺ the Sum of
Ten pounds 3/9 for the Ufe and Service of the **State** of *Maſſachuſetts-Bay*, and in Behalf
of faid **State** I do hereby promiſe and oblige Myſelf and Succeſſors in the Office of
Treaſurer, to repay to the faid Jeremiah Smith
or Bearer, by the Firſt Day of March, A. D. 1782, the aforeſaid Sum of
Ten pounds Three shillings
with Intereſt Annually at **Six** per Cent. per Annum.

1934

J. Holley
Eza price
Boyer

Committee

Witneſs my Hand.

H. Gardner Treaſurer

COUNTERFEIT THIS.

DEATH TO

MASSACHUSETTS TREASURY CERTIFICATE, 1777

The United States has paid for wars with money it did not have since the American Revolution. How does a government spend more money than the revenue raised? In some ways the answer has not changed. The Iraq war contributes to a deficit that must be closed through bond issues. Bondholders presently, however, feel assured of the promised return on their investment. Today, a security issued by the United States government stands among the safest investments available. As the nation fought for its independence, however, confidence in redeeming a bond's face value seemed far from assured.

The bond shown here was a Massachusetts Treasury certificate dated December 1, 1777. Representing ten pounds, thirteen shillings, it accrued 6 percent interest upon maturity in March 1782. Massachusetts had issued this particular certificate to consolidate its accumulated debt. The exigencies of war led the state to issue bills of credit in exchange for goods and services. Lacking an adequate amount of specie, or hard money, Massachusetts's bills of credit stood as IOUs to people whose goods were confiscated or who offered services required. Used as paper money, they did not carry interest because the bearer expected redemption shortly. As paper money often did, their value declined quickly. The state replaced this assortment of bills of credit by exchanging them for treasury notes, such as the one shown here. Not only did this consolidate the loan, it extended the payment due date—thus, the need for 6 percent interest. Since the state exchanged these notes for already borrowed money, the inscription began with "Received of" rather than "Borrowed and Received of" as other state treasury receipts did.

Paul Revere designed and engraved this note. Revere's business as silversmith and copper engraver, and his close connection with the Massachusetts leadership, also led to his designing the Massachusetts colonial seal and its first colonial currency, created to pay soldiers. The rattlesnake encircling a pine tree in the upper left hand corner of this treasury note were familiar symbols to Massachusetts citizens at the time. The snake often represented unity. American colonists first saw it segmented into eight pieces in Benjamin Franklin's 1754 *Pennsylvania Gazette* political cartoon, "Join, or Die." Franklin appealed to the colonies to unite into a confederation in anticipation of the French and Indian War. While Franklin's snake was not a rattler, later Paul Revere used a rattlesnake on his design of the masthead of a Patriot newspaper, the *Massachusetts Spy*, as a symbol of unity for the cause. The rattlesnake iconography continued to represent Patriot unity on several subsequent occasions. A rattlesnake with the motto, "Don't tread on me" began to be used throughout the colonies on flags and currency. It also became the symbol of the American navy.

Trees had iconic significance to Massachusetts citizens also, since they had come to symbolize liberty in the public mind. According to David Hackett Fischer in *Liberty and Freedom*, that association dates to earlier English history. He writes that trees "symbolized ancient folk-rights of freedom and liberty." Massachusetts had adopted the pine tree, such as the one on this bond, early in its existence, using it on their pine tree shillings in 1652. Of course, the Liberty Tree evolved into an important political symbol. Andrew Oliver's effigy hung from Deacon Jacob Elliot's elm, which became known as the Liberty Elm, at the beginning of the Stamp Act crisis in 1765.

Jeremiah Smith originally received this note. Although many Smiths populated Lexington at the time, particularly in the southern part, no Jeremiahs exist in Charles Hudson's genealogies or in vital records. How the Lexington Historical Society came to possess the note remains unclear. John Scollay, Peter Boyer and Ezekial Price, designated as a "committee," signed the note along with the treasurer of Massachusetts Bay, Henry Gardner.

Bonds such as these became central to class-based disputes, both at the state and national level, in subsequent years. Due to uncertainty about the state's solvency, speculators often purchased securities at a discount, hoping to later redeem them at a higher value than paid. By 1781 their value, according to Leonard L. Richards in *Shays's Rebellion*, had plummeted to one-fortieth their face value. In the early 1780s the Massachusetts legislature, a body dominated by the mercantile interest, decided to repay the state's $5 million debt in notes at face value. Bond values had fluctuated as rapidly in other states once severe inflation became a byproduct of the war. But these states had not taken a position that so clearly favored the wealthy. Most states were redeeming at their present worth, not face value. Richards notes that Virginia paid one-thousandth the face value and the central government funded its notes at one-fortieth their value at that stage.

The Massachusetts approach favored merchants who also by then held most of the bonds. Richards points out that the thirty-five largest investors in bonds owned 40 percent of their value. All thirty-five sat in the legislature or had a close relative who did. Taxes had to be raised to fund the Massachusetts debt. The system fell hardest on poor farmers because taxes on land were much heavier than on moveable property. Two-thirds of the debt came from land taxes and one-third from the rest. Farmers asked for paper money issues so as to pay the taxes more easily—they hoped through their devaluation—but were denied.

Farmers west of Lexington had been agitating against the economic policies in 1781–82, closing courts in Pittsfield so that they could not process foreclosures or confiscate property for unpaid taxes. Finally, open rebellion erupted in 1786 led by Daniel Shays, a former officer in the American Revolution. The Rebels closed several Court of Common Pleas or debtors courts, including those in Northampton and Worcester. The militia in the western counties had proved too sympathetic to the Rebel cause so merchants funded an army of 4,400 to put down the Rebels. The militia did take part. Hudson's genealogies notes that Lexington's Colonel William Munroe of the militia, formerly Captain Parker's orderly sergeant, had marched toward Springfield in 1786. The militia's mission was to seize its arsenal before Shays's Rebels did.

However this note came into the possession of the Lexington Historical Society, it probably changed hands several times at prices that fluctuated, but never approached face value. Certainly if the value of our bonds today were as unsure, foreign countries would not be so avidly purchasing our debt.

Name	No. Polls	Poll Tax	Personal Estate	Real Estate	Sum total Whole Tax	Town Tax	County Tax
Benjamin Loth	1	38	0..21	1..18	1 X 77	6 X 20	0 X 53
Phill. Munro	1	38	0..15	0..46	0..X 99	3..X 47	0..X 30
Willia Munro s	1	38	0..15	0..46	0..X 99	34 47	0..X 30
Heni John William	1		0..7	0..61	0..X 68	2..X 36	0 X 20
Stephen Robbins	3	14	3..85	1..36	6 X 35	22 X 23	1 X 91
Thaddeus Reed	1	38	0..43	2..48	3..X 29	11 X 52	0..X 99
Ohn. W. Eastabrook	2	76	0..62	4..50	5 X 88	21..X 37	1 X 76
Nathan Ruggell	1	X 38	0..48	2..53	3 X 39	11..X 07	1 X 2
Nathan Jefferson	1	38	0..34	1..20	1 X 92	6..X 72	0 X 58
Jonas Ruggell	1	38	0..29	0..63	1 X 24	4..X 34	0 X 37
Abijah Wymor	1	38	0..18	1..5	1 X 61	5..X 61	0 X 48
Samuel Simonds	1	38	0..80	0..20	1 X 46	5 X 11	0 X 44
Joseph Simonds Jun.	1	X 8	0..0	3..49	3 X 87	13 X 55	1 X 16
The Toronia Totly Rogers by Dorris Shaw				0.. 23	0 X 23	0..X 81	0..X 7

TAX ASSESSMENT BOOK 1800

Many political debates today center on tax policy. Who likes to pay taxes? They are, according to Winston Churchill, "The price we pay for civilization." But people disagree on what constitutes this "civilization." Disputes abound over the amount of revenue government requires, the services it should provide and whether services are delivered in a cost-efficient manner. This is not unlike the disputes of the past. None were more mindful of the importance of tax policy than the citizens of Lexington in 1800. They had just fought a war in which tax policy figured prominently as a cause. At the turn of the nineteenth century they paid taxes mostly to the state, county and local governments, federal income taxes being forbidden by the new Constitution. Yankee farmers preferred paying taxes to governments close at hand. That does not mean they liked it.

Shown here is a page from the Lexington tax assessment book for 1800. The town collected state and county taxes, as well as town, usually in one bill. As shown, the last three columns list the taxes levied by these three governments. These taxes were identical to those collected by towns in Massachusetts when still a colony, excluding of course, those imposed by Parliament at issue before the Revolution. Once independence came, the provincial tax simply became the state tax. As shown, three taxes made up the state levy, set by the state legislature. A poll tax was one, in this case thirty-eight cents for males in the household over sixteen years old and eligible to register for military service. In the case of Stephen Robbins (fifth from the top), who shows three polls, the other two were probably his two oldest sons, Stephen, twenty, and Samuel, nineteen. Only men were assessed, so many of the households show only one poll. The state placed limits on poll tax rates, only one-fifth of its total taxes via the poll tax, since citizens must pay the tax to vote.

The other five-sixths came from a tax on property, both moveable and land. Unlike the regressive poll tax, property taxes were progressive—the wealthiest paid the most. The value of land and buildings owned made up the real estate tax, while the tax on personal estate included moveable property such as carriages, livestock, personal income, slaves, grains, cider, etc. Stephen Robbins, who had established his fur-dressing business in East Lexington by 1800, had acquired the largest personal estate on this page. No doubt his store and fur-dressing buildings were part of the levy. Land was taxed according to the use of the land, such as woodland, meadow, tillage, etc. In contrast to Robbins, Attia Estabrook (seventh from the top) inherited at least part of his father Benjamin Estabrook's land on the north side of Massachusetts Avenue in center village, and paid higher taxes on real estate. Only thirty-one at the time of the assessment, he had not acquired much personal property. Perhaps the same could be said of Joseph Simonds Jr. (third from the bottom), who was only twenty-nine at the time.

The town assessors compiled the tax book. In 1800 Isaac Winship, Jonathan Harrington Jr. and Joseph Simonds Jr. served as assessors. The x's crossed between the dollars and cents in the totals columns probably recorded payment in full. Assessors also made abatements for town residents unable to pay their taxes, such as widows. Town meeting could also do this. Who collected the taxes? Early in colonial Massachusetts's history the constable collected taxes as part of his duties, which also included announcing upcoming town meetings and serving writs for the town clerk. Often the first elected position for a young man, the constable received a commission for the taxes he collected. There was, however, a catch. He was also responsible for taxes not collected. In Boston half the taxes had to be paid in the first three months and the second half in the next three months. Towns sued tax collectors in arrears for payment. The most famous tax collector who found himself in financial difficulty due to being delinquent in collecting taxes was Sam Adams.

Since the office of constable had its drawbacks, it became difficult to find men who would accept the office if elected. One might be excused from elected office for a good reason or a fee. In 1733 Boston separated the tax collecting duties from the constable, creating the job of tax collector. By 1800 Lexington had done the same. Amos Muzzey Jr. was constable, while Nathan Munroe had the unenviable task of collecting taxes, with a commission of "twelve cents on the pound." In all likelihood tax collecting in Lexington, especially during good economic times, proved financially far less risky than in Boston. Even so, John Mulliken and Nathan Chandler as insurance bonded Munroe.

Where did the money go? The county tax supported the court system and the state tax provided for state government functions, such as funding the state militia. The effect of town taxes could be seen every day. Part of Massachusetts's town taxes supported the schools. Town records show that in March 1800 the Lexington selectmen paid Joshua Reed $30.67 for boarding the schoolmaster for sixteen weeks in the northwest district. The town paid Nathan Reed for a cord of wood to heat the school. In another district, Thomas Fessenden earned $20.63 for "keeping school for seven weeks in Southwest district." Town coffers still supported the church in 1800. Jonas Smith received $21.26 "for cutting and carting the Rev. Mr. [Clarke's] wood."

The town tax funded poor relief for worthy town residents. The worthy poor included suddenly destitute widows, so long as they were established residents. Robert Parker boarded the widow Fessenden for an entire year. Town tax revenue reimbursed him for $66 on August 4, 1800. A form of Medicaid was also in place. On May 12 the town agreed with Doctor David Fiske that he would "Docter all the poor" for one year for fourteen dollars. Public funds also maintained town buildings. Nathan Dudley earned $14 for maintaining the meetinghouse and ringing the bell for a year. While work on the highway was paid in labor, Jonathan Robinson was paid $3.31 as highway surveyor.

No doubt many Lexingtonians grumbled about taxes in 1800, even if its effects could be seen close to home. This seems to be a complaint not bound by chronological barriers. It is timeless.

This Indenture

Witnesseth, That _Abner Stone an orphan now aged nineteen years eight months and seven days_

HATH put himself, and by these presents, by and with the advice and consent of _two of the Special Justices for preserving the peace in the city of New York_

DOTH voluntarily, and of his own free will and accord, put himself Apprentice to _William Buckley_ of the City and State of New-York, _Brass founder_ to learn the Art, Trade, and Mystery of _a Brass founder_ and after the manner of an Apprentice to serve from the day of the date hereof, for and during, and until the full end and term of _One year three months and twenty three days_

next ensuing: During all which time, the said Apprentice his Master faithfully shall serve, his secrets keep, his lawful commands every where readily obey: he shall do no damage to his said Master, nor see it done by others, without letting or giving notice thereof to his said Master: he must not contract matrimony within the said term: he shall not waste his said Master's goods, nor lend them unlawfully to any; at cards, dice, or any unlawful game, he shall not play, whereby his said Master may have damage: he shall neither traffic with his own goods, nor the goods of others, nor shall he buy or sell, without license from his said Master: he shall not absent himself day nor night from his Master's service, without his leave: nor haunt ale-houses, taverns or play-houses, but in all things behave himself as a faithful Apprentice ought to do, during the said term. AND the said Master shall use the utmost of his endeavours to teach, or cause to be taught, or instructed, the said Apprentice, in the Trade or Mystery of _a Brass founder_ and procure and provide for him sufficient _work at the business_

fitting for an Apprentice, during the said term of _service — And in lieu of boarding pay two dollars & fifty cents weekly, and in lieu of clothing pay twenty five dollars yearly in quarterly payments — also give him a quarters evening schooling in each year —_

AND for the true performance of all and singular the covenants and agreements aforesaid, the said parties bind themselves each unto the other firmly by these presents. IN WITNESS WHEREOF, the said parties have interchangeably set their hands and seals hereunto, at the City of New-York, the _twenty seventh_ day of _August_ in the _56_ year of the Independence of the United States of America, and in the year of our Lord one thousand eight hundred and thirty _one —_

SEALED AND DELIVERED IN THE PRESENCE OF

R. Stephens

No. 171 Bowery

William Buckley

Abner Stone

We the undersigned Special Justices for preserving the peace in the city of New York certify that we Consent to the above binding of the orphan

John M. Wyman

James Hopson

ABNER STONE'S INDENTURE CONTRACT, 1831

More easily than today, fortunes could rise and fall sharply in the nineteenth century. The trajectory of Lexington's Abner Stone's life presents an excellent example. In 1851 he was successful enough to purchase the building that would bear his name before becoming East Lexington Branch Library. His life did not begin with such promise.

The Stone family in 1635 emigrated from Great Bromley in Essex County, England, one of the original families that settled in New Towne, now Cambridge. Charles Hudson in his genealogies in the *History of Lexington Volume II* notes that the Stones settled in the western part of Cambridge, partly in what later became Lexington, and partly in what became Lincoln. So many members of Stone extended family lived in the area that Hudson writes, "They were designated in the records according to their geographical position, as John Stone, East and John Stone, West, Samuel Stone, East and Samuel Stone, West."

Over time the fortunes of the once prominent family seems to have foundered. Hudson notes in the first edition of his *History* that the family "seems to have disappeared so suddenly, and to have left a record so imperfect that it is impossible to state...the place to where they were removed." According to Edwin Worthen in *Retracing Lexington's Past*, they had "rather gone to seed" He conjectured, "Liquor and debts probably the reason." What he based this on remains unclear. Did he offer those reasons because they were typical explanations for a family's decline? Or had he some information about the Stones that has since been lost? Regardless, when Samuel Stone died on New Year's Day in 1830, his son Abner appeared to possess few options for support. The oldest of five children, he was nineteen at the time. His biological mother had died earlier and his father had remarried. But he did not stay with his stepmother. Soon after he entered an indenture contract, as an orphan, to apprentice as a brass founder in New York City. The master he was bound to, William Buckley, lived in the Bowery section of the city. It was not unusual to apprentice a young man of his age and circumstances. But why was he not apprenticed somewhere closer to Lexington? Why had he ended up in New York? The answer to these questions and many others are unknown. But some information about Abner Stone can be inferred.

Often poor relief overseers of the town "bound out" orphans to an apprenticeship; otherwise they may be a charge of the town. It saved the town money and taught a skill to give the child a start in life. But it is doubtful Lexington would have arranged a New York City apprenticeship. And with the stepmother still alive, it seems even less likely. So how Abner ended up in New York City remains a mystery. Abner signed the indenture agreement almost eight months after his father's death. Since he was the only sibling who was not the biological child of his stepmother, she or a blood relative might have arranged it. Abner Stone may have come to New York City to stay with a relative, then entered into the agreement. But that seems unlikely since he is referred to as an orphan—without even a guardian at the time.

The terms of the contract present no mystery, however. First, in 1831 Abner Stone, the contract stipulates, is apprenticed to William Buckley, to be taught "the trade or mystery of brass founder." As a brass founder, Abner learned to melt brass and bronze to pour into molds to make andirons, bells, shoe buckles, sword hilts and similar products. It was hot and dirty work. William Buckley lived at 171 Bowery Street. This lively entertainment sector of New York teemed with dance halls, rowdy theaters, saloons and performing animals. It is likely Buckley felt at home among his Irish counterparts there. The largest influx of Irish, however, came about fifteen years later. It only became rougher in later years, spawning gangs by the 1850s.

Abner's obligations involved doing what he was told and staying out of trouble. Buckley's obligations included providing room, clothes, board and teaching a marketable skill. This particular contract offered considerable autonomy. Instead of Buckley supplying room and board, it specifies the amount he would pay Stone, "two dollars and fifty cents weekly," for arranging his own board. Buckley also paid twenty-five dollars per year for clothes and paid for evening school. Perhaps this autonomy came because Stone was nineteen. Still, it must have been a rude awakening to live and work in New York's Bowery section in 1831 after having spent your first nineteen years in a rural town. When he reached twenty-one, the contract released Abner from his legal obligations. Until then an indenture functioned as a form of servitude. The apprentice could not break it. Runaway apprentices would be returned if found. But unlike a slave, an apprentice could not be sold or assigned to another.

When and how Abner Stone found his way back to Lexington remains another question without documentary answers. Edwin Worthen speculated that Stone went to work for Eli Robbins at some point. Worthen also writes that Abner became a financial success in St. Louis. The sequence of these two events remains unclear. But documentation exists for some events. By 1851 Stone's affluence enabled him to purchase Robbins Hall. Three years later he married Ellen Robbins. They married in Hartford, Connecticut. Worthen speculated that the couple chose this distant venue because the family did not approve of the marriage. He offers no evidence, so it may have been pure speculation. Ellen's diary reveals ambivalence about marrying Abner right up to the end. The diary stops one month before the marriage, and she still is pondering whether she should marry Abner. Regardless of the reason for the Hartford marriage, the couple returned to be near Lexington. Their daughter was born in 1854 in the old homestead now occupied by Aunt Caira. Town tax records do not reveal the Stones having a residence in Lexington. But Abner's account book does list monthly payments to Eli Robbins for board, so at least for the first several years the newlyweds lived with Ellen's parents. During the early part of their marriage the couple lived at times in St. Louis, perhaps to more closely tend to his business interests there.

In some ways Eli Robbins's life followed an opposite trajectory. During the early part of the 1830s he was East Lexington's leading man. But in 1837 his business went bankrupt due to the financial panic of 1837. He was forced to sell much of his property by order of the Middlesex County sheriff. A handbill exists in the archives that advertises an auction of a lot of Robbins's moveable property including twelve to fifteen thousand skins, two horses, a carriage, wagon and chaise. Certainly the sale of the Robbins building should be seen in that light.

In contrast Abner Stone died a far wealthier man than he began—an orphan bound out to a brass worker in one of the roughest sections of New York City. He became reasonably wealthy, married into East

Lexington's most prominent family and owned an important building that would carry his name. As a final legacy, his daughter, Ellen Stone, would remain an influential East Villager into the 1940s. Not bad for a destitute orphan boy.

COMMONWEALTH OF MASSACHUSETTS.

This Certifies, that on the 25th day of October A.D. 1823
Jonas Munroe was admitted into the

Middlesex Society

of HUSBANDMEN and MANUFACTURERS;

and is entitled to all the rights and privileges of a
MEMBER thereof.

S. Brooks Secretary.

David Lawrence President.

MEMBERSHIP CERTIFICATE TO THE MIDDLESEX COUNTY SOCIETY OF HUSBANDMEN AND MANUFACTURERS, 1823

As with most towns in Middlesex County, Lexington began as an agricultural community and remained so for most of its history. Although only a combined twenty-five acres of the Busa and Wilson farms remain under tillage in town today, Lexington's development has not completely eradicated traces of its former rural status. The amount of green space that remains makes it not so difficult to imagine a farming town in the early nineteenth century.

Lexington's close proximity to Boston led its farmers to take advantage of the city's market after early nineteenth-century advances in infrastructure made daily trips into Boston practical. These former subsistence farmers began to market commodities to the urban population, including produce and dairy products. By the 1820s milk producers such as Nathaniel Pierce and Benjamin Wellington rose at midnight to deliver milk to Charlestown, Cambridge and Boston. As Boston's closest suburbs—Brookline, Roxbury and Jamaica Plain—increased in population and other commercial opportunities, by the 1840s market gardens were pushed further out to Watertown, Newton and Arlington. Lexington had also begun to move toward market gardening with the 1850s as its transitional decade.

Once involved in commercial agriculture, Lexington farmers took a keen interest in improving their methodology—but were cautious in approaching experimentation. As the nineteenth century began, the rationalism of the Enlightenment had influenced agriculture toward a more scientific approach.

This appreciation of "scientific agriculture" led to the creation of America's first state agricultural society in 1794: The Massachusetts Society for the Promotion of Agriculture. The Society's creators and promoters, however, were the Boston elite—gentlemen farmers by avocation. Lexington's own gentleman farmer, Elias Phinney, court clerk in Cambridge by vocation, took an active role in the MSPA. He served as secretary while promoting several innovations on his Spring Street farm.

Middlesex County members of the MSPA also set out to organize at the county level as soon as the MSPA began. The Middlesex organization, like the statewide, rewarded innovation by offering premiums in the form of cash prizes for categories of produce, livestock, inventions and home manufacture at its annual Cattle Show and Exhibition (also called the Agricultural Fair) first held in 1820. Usually held in September, the gathering took place in several Middlesex locations, but primarily in Concord, the county seat. This exhibit enabled the organization to celebrate progressive techniques and to sharpen the region's competitive edge. As befits the time, its motto read, "Agriculture is the leading interest of nations." First called the Western Society of Middlesex Husbandmen in 1794, an act of the Massachusetts legislature in 1820 added "and Manufacturers" and dropped "Western." The Concord Library's special collections house the manuscript records of the Society. They make interesting reading.

Shown here is Jonas Munroe's membership certificate. He became one of the first Lexington residents to join the organization. Known as proprietor of Munroe Tavern, his farm encompassed the Tavern grounds and extended up the hill. He was indeed a husbandman. Middlesex farmers practiced mixed husbandry—combining the cultivation of produce and raising livestock.

Not only did the Society promote agricultural experimentation through premiums, it also wanted to improve home manufacture. The home manufacture category demonstrated the importance of the farmer's wife. Home products such as glassware and needlework won premiums, but cloth was most prized. At this stage of the nineteenth century women still produced homespun. In 1822 seventy-one Middlesex participants entered the competition, although none from Lexington. The next year the town's lone entry was from Mary Harrington. Lydia A. Brown entered for a coverlet and Laura Hosmer (age twelve) for lace in 1829. No man from Lexington entered during those years. While Lexington farmers belonged to the county organization, especially early in the Society's existence, the town's representation was small. Two possible reasons might explain this.

Many farmers viewed the county organizations as elitist at first. The Secretary's Report of the Massachusetts Board of Agriculture in 1852 looked back at the early years. It noted, "All the County Societies previous to 1820, suffered much from unjust criticism and ridicule of the class they were designed to benefit." Part of this can be explained by skepticism toward "book farming." Many farmers looked askance at learning about scientific innovation from those who did not work the land as a livelihood. For the practicing farmers, academics could not improve upon knowing what they knew through actual work. But this attitude would change.

Another reason for the meager initial participation in the Society's activities could be owed to the organization's purpose: to improve practice through experimentation. Lexington was a pretty poor town on average and experimentation often required taking risks. Most of the town's farmers could ill afford to lose crop or livestock to a failed experiment.

Jonas Munroe, Abijah Harrington, Oliver Locke, Jonas Bridge, Amos Muzzey Jr., Charles Reed and Nathaniel Cutler all received membership diplomas on October 2, 1823, the date on Munroe's diploma. What do these men have in common? Although reasonably prosperous, others enjoyed similar or more prosperity. The answer might be found in their record of public service. Actively involved in civic leadership, it could be argued that they were representing the town in this new capacity— promoting agricultural innovation, advancing the interests of the town. Harrington, Bridge, Muzzey, Reed and Cutler had all served terms as selectmen in previous years. Oliver Locke had been assessor and captain of the militia. Only Jonas Munroe had not held public office. But as proprietor of the Munroe Tavern, he had interest in the economic health of the town.

Lexington began to take a larger role in the Society in ensuing years. Reverend Charles Briggs made the keynote speech in 1825 at the annual exhibition. Two Society presidents lived in Lexington: Elias Phinney (1831), of course, and Samuel Chandler (1853). Like the MSPA, presidents were men of some stature. Chandler was county sheriff for ten years and served as state senator. Phinney's experimental work with Ayeshire cattle and produce was so well known that people came from a distance to observe his farm.

Interest among Lexington farmers increased in ensuing years. Records of the premiums awarded show Lexingtonians, while not dominant, held their own. In 1853 C.W. Joslin won one dollar for potatoes and peaches and Bowen Harrington four dollars for celery. Three years later Johnson and Harrington won again, both for a bushel of wheat that must have been quite notable. But also Andrew Wellington won six dollars for a bull. Under the needlework and manufacture category Joseph Fisk won a one-dollar prize for a shell table he constructed.

Over the years Lexington farmers continued to belong to organizations that helped advance their practice, such as the Grange and later the Farm Bureau. Sadly, most Lexington farmers, who had for generations adapted to challenges they faced, succumbed to economic and demographic forces that overwhelmed any powers to adapt. Competition caused by transportation advances, agribusiness competition and federal regulations eventually led to most farms selling for development or becoming conservation land. Still, it is not difficult to imagine Lexington as a landscape covered with farms.

Certificate, No. ____

LEXINGTON & WEST CAMBRIDGE
RAILROAD COMPANY.

Be it Known, That *Jonas Moore* of *Lexington* of *Lexington* Shares ____ is the Proprietor of *Two* ____

in the **Capital Stock** of the **Lexington & West-Cambridge Railroad Company,** subject to the Provisions of the Charter, and the By-Laws of the Corporation, the same being transferable by an assignment thereof in the Books of said Corporation, and when a Transfer shall be made, and this Certificate surrendered, a new Certificate or new Certificates will be issued.

Dated at Boston, this *18* day of *June* ____ A.D. 18*49*

Benjamin Muggs President.

Wm Hovel Treasurer.

INCOR. MAR. 24. 1845. LEXINGTON & W.C. RAIL ROAD CO

LEXINGTON & WEST CAMBRIDGE RAILROAD.

JONAS MUNROE'S RAILROAD STOCK CERTIFICATE, 1847

Runners, walkers, bicyclers, cross-country skiers and in-line skaters who use the Minuteman bike path either to commute or for recreation owe a tremendous debt to those who founded the Lexington and West Cambridge Railroad in 1846. The track now covered in asphalt laid the course that so many people have used daily since it opened in 1992. Little did the enterprising men who financed the route imagine that more than 150 years later, future residents would travel over their railroad in such a variety of ways. These men, led by Benjamin Muzzey, motivated by both self and public interest, had a vastly different idea for its use. Ultimately, they succeeded, connecting Lexington to Cambridge and Boston, and changing the town forever.

Interest in a railroad link from Lexington to the city can be traced to early nineteenth-century transportation advances and their effect on the tavern business. Caught on the wrong side of this new age were the tavern proprietors along Lexington's Main Street, today Massachusetts Avenue. Buckman Tavern, Dudley Tavern, Monument House, Munroe Tavern and Cutler Tavern, among others, had previously benefited from the traditional commercial traffic that crowded Massachusetts Avenue, the main road to Boston. Carts and pungs drawn by teams of four and six horses or oxen laden with produce from northern Massachusetts, New Hampshire and Vermont farms needed rest stops. Taverns along the route offered overnight accommodations as well as a stop for refreshments. In addition, cattle, sheep and other livestock were driven through the same streets. Some taverns, such as Munroe's, allowed for grazing during a drover's respite on the way to the Brighton stockyards. Turnpikes, canals and later railroads became the conduit for what would later be called the commercial revolution by shipping goods to market more cheaply.

Benjamin Muzzey owned Monument House, the largest hotel in town, built by his father Amos in 1805. The tavern stood in the present location of CVS. The Muzzey family also owned the homestead near where the Edison building now stands, along with back land from Merriam Street to Grant Street up to Granny Hill. The tavern business was a Muzzey tradition. An earlier member of the family, John Muzzey, built Buckman Tavern around 1709. When the Middlesex Canal was built in 1803 and a few years later the Middlesex and Concord Turnpikes opened, Benjamin Muzzey began to grow uneasy. The alternative canal and turnpike routes redirected traffic from the center, threatening his business. Other taverns had sprung up along the turnpikes and prospered. Muzzey wanted to change that.

Railroads were the wave of the future at the time. By 1835 railroads from Boston to Worcester, Lowell and Providence began service. The Boston and Lowell Railroad had effectively diverted commerce from the Middlesex Canal. The Fitchburg Railroad opened in 1843, extending from Charlestown to Waltham. By 1844 businessmen of West Cambridge, today Arlington, began to organize to build a railroad. The seven mills in West Cambridge stood to benefit from a route to the city. Once alerted, Muzzey began to organize in Lexington. When both groups petitioned for a charter of incorporation, the state legislature compromised by merging the two railroads into one—thus, the name Lexington and West Cambridge Railroad.

After meeting at Cutler's Tavern, the site of Arlex Oil today, on April 14, 1845, to accept the legislature's act of incorporation, a committee formed to raise money through stock subscriptions, with Benjamin Muzzey elected chairman of this committee. Fittingly, he had earlier been elected president of the railroad. Jonas Munroe, proprietor of Munroe Tavern, a Massachusetts Avenue establishment that stood to benefit from commerce's redirection though the center of town, owned the stock certificate shown here. He purchased ten shares on June 18, 1847, about a year after the railroad was incorporated. Each share cost $100 each for a total of $1,000. This was no insignificant investment. Corrected for inflation, it would be worth approximately $20,000 today. At the time of the stock purchase, Benjamin Muzzey served as president and William Stevens had become treasurer. Muzzey died the following year and was succeeded by Charles W. Warren and then Charles Hudson as president.

The railroad's first run began on August 25, 1846. This early railroad featured a locomotive called the Muzzey (it was customary to name locomotives as one would ships) pulling two secondhand passenger cars and a baggage car on a single track to the brickyard in Cambridge, today Fresh Pond. Once there, passengers waited for a train to Boston on the Fitchburg Railroad. Amos Locke was the first conductor and the engineer was John Peters, born in Germany, both of Lexington. In anticipation of the increased commercial activity a railroad would bring to the center village, Benjamin Muzzey built Lexington House in 1847 on the site of his Monument House—a year after the opening of the railroad. Located near the center depot, the Muzzey's Hotel, its first name, could capitalize on business from railroad travelers. The railroad was double tracked in 1885. At its height there were five depot stations in Lexington. But by then the railroad had changed hands.

In 1865 David W. Muzzey, Benjamin's son and president, published a bulletin announcing most of the stock as worthless. This included Munroe's. Jonas Munroe had passed away, but his estate took the $1,000 loss. During the Civil War the renamed Lexington and Arlington Railroad suffered financially, leading to bankruptcy. In 1870 Boston and Lowell Railroad absorbed it. The Boston and Lowell in turn was absorbed by the Boston and Maine in 1887.

A list of those owning original stock purchases show a number of Lexington, Arlington and Boston residents, as well as several other Massachusetts towns. These residents took large losses. David W. Muzzey himself, no doubt inheritor of Benjamin Muzzey's shares, held 250 at the time. Charles Hudson, former congressman and author of *History of Lexington, Massachusetts* held 42. East Lexington resident Otis Dana had 61 and his daughter Ellen 5. Ellen inherited her grandfather's Greek revival home on Massachusetts Avenue and later left her estate to the Lexington Home for Aged People, now the Dana Home on Massachusetts Avenue near Worthen Road.

The railroad lived on, however, not closing until 1977. Its impact on the town in the nineteenth century was critical. It not only led to an increase in population, but it brought a whole new class of Lexington residents—ones with business interests in the city. Those who use the path today might pause to remember its roots.

Know all Men by these Presents,

That I, Isaac N. Damon, of Lexington, County of Middlesex and State of Massachusetts, Treasurer of the **FIRST CONGREGATIONAL SOCIETY**, in said Lexington; by virtue of the Statute Laws of this Commonwealth, and in consideration of *One Hundred & five* ———— Dollars paid by *John Marett* ———— the receipt whereof I do hereby acknowledge, do hereby grant, sell, and convey, to the said *John Marett. His* heirs and assigns for ever, Pew No. *Sixty-one* in the House of Public Worship erected by a Vote of said First Congregational Society, being numbered *Sixty-one* that being bought at a public auction of the Pews in said House, and the highest price offered for the same.

To Have and to Hold the said Pew, with all the privileges and appurtenances thereto belonging, and secured by the general Laws of the Commonwealth, to the said *John Marett. His* ———— heirs and assigns to and for *His & their* use and benefit for ever.

In Witness Whereof, I, the said Isaac N. Damon, *as Treasurer* - do hereto set my hand and seal, this *Third* ———— day of *August* in the year one thousand eight hundred and *Forty-eight* ————

Signed, Sealed, and Delivered,
in presence of us,

Lucy H Damon

Chester Mann

Isaac N. Damon, Treasurer.

Middlesex ss. *August 21st* A.D. 18*40* Then the said Isaac N. Damon in his capacity of Treasurer, personally appeared and acknowledged this instrument to be his deed.

Before me,

William Chandler Justice of the Peace.

JOHN MARRETT'S PEW DEED
1848

Selecting a seat in a church seems to be such a simple process today that the idea of reserving one through actually owning a pew puzzles one at first. But then the idea of owning season tickets to a sporting event comes to mind—not a perfect analogy by any means, but with some similar elements. Regardless, the inevitable questions do arise. Why would anyone buy a church pew location? How would selling them benefit a church? The answers, of course, lie in the traditions, values and realities of the time period.

As with any colonial Congregational parish, a committee determined the seating arrangement in Lexington's first meetinghouse. A monument behind the Captain Parker statue marks its location on the Common. A one-story structure built in 1694 when Lexington was still a precinct of Cambridge, the arrangement segregated males and females on long benches separated by the center aisle. Social position and age factored into how close one sat to the front. Girls sat with their mothers and boys sat together in the back under the watchful eye of the tythingmen. The congregation began to seat families together after it built the second meetinghouse in 1714. This structure accommodated its parishioners with a combination of pews along the walls and benches filling the middle of the floor. Pews were sold to members once the committee had determined the plan. Pew sales raised important revenue for the church—especially the seed money to build the meetinghouse. But that revenue was limited since the floor plan devoted so little space to pews. At the time, town tax revenue funded Massachusetts Congregational churches. This continued into the nineteenth century. Non-pew owners sat where specified by the seating committee on the benches that filled the middle of the room. Two galleries provided further capacity, with the upper one occupied by poor, slaves and rowdy boys.

The seating committee's work appeared to be a thankless one. It requested the ages of all congregants so as to weigh age and status. While Puritan/Congregational New England's culture was more egalitarian than many other regions, especially the South, congregants remained mindful of status. Thus, Sunday meeting was not simply a religious event. Attending meeting was the one occasion when virtually the entire town gathered under one roof, placing the town's social structure on full display. Consequently, the seating committee dealt with complaints from families claiming to be located below their station. In 1744 town meeting itself rejected the committee's work. Also, because of in and out migration, seating arrangements required reconfiguration periodically, further complicating the seating dynamic.

This second meetinghouse was sited on the Common farther west than the first while facing east. This meetinghouse obscured the view of the British as they approached the militia in Lexington in 1775. As seen in the Doolittle engraving, still a multipurpose building, the meetinghouse looked more like a large house than a church. The town even stored its munitions in the gallery. As the British approached the Common on April 19, 1775, four militia entered the meetinghouse for ammunition. Caleb Harrington was killed as he exited the building.

The third meetinghouse, built in 1794 still farther northwest on the Common, looked like a modern-day church. But it was painted pea green. Although still box-like, it included a steeple with a bell tower, as well as three entrances with porches. The front faced Buckman Tavern. Stone posts and horseblocks accommodated the horses and carriages of congregants traveling from a distance. This time pews were auctioned, not assigned, to the highest bidder. Perhaps the republican spirit of the age influenced the removal of traditional deference to social position. As Joyce Appleby points out in *Inheriting the Revolution*, the years following the Revolution made "an egalitarian society disencumbered by privilege" the goal of the next generation. If pew auctions had egalitarian motives, they failed miserably. Status still determined seating, since congregants with the most money purchased the most desirable locations. Pew sales funded the meetinghouse's construction and auctioning them certainly brought a higher price. This church devoted the entire floor plan to pews. The owners constructed their pews after purchasing the space. Fifty-four pews were auctioned for a total of $6,129.47. A gallery loomed on three sides, with the poor sitting on the gallery's periphery. Gallery pews were also sold, accruing an additional $856.50. The pew's number and the owner's name stood out in these paneled pews. Metal rails finished their tops. The deacons' pews stood in the front, below the raised pulpit, facing the congregation. A pew's expense did not end the owner's financial obligation. Since it carried a deed showing ownership, the church assessed its value each year to charge a property tax.

When the third meetinghouse burned in 1846, just after an expensive remodeling, plans for a fourth church began immediately. A vote carried on February 15, 1847, to build a new church for a cost not to exceed $8,000. But this meetinghouse departed from past practice in several ways. With a town hall built the same year, this building served exclusively as a church. Also, in a controversial decision, the church was sited off the Common. It rose in the lot purchased from Bowen Harrington where it still stands today on Harrington Road. The church auctioned pews to pay for the building and constructed twenty-one horse stables behind it.

By this time the church no longer received town tax revenue. In 1833 Massachusetts discontinued public funding of what were called Standing Order churches—the original Congregational churches. The variety of sects now competing with them made a state-funded church untenable. Although in 1819 the First Parish had become Unitarian, it still enjoyed the monopoly on town funds as well as revenue from sales of ministerial land. The money from the ministerial land sales now had to be divided with East Lexington's church, the Baptist church and the later Hancock Church. Consequently, pew auctions carried more importance since funding became more reliant on the church membership.

John Marrett purchased pew sixty-one in the fourth meetinghouse on August 3, 1848. The deed is shown here. Ownership carried the right to transfer the property through sale or to bequeath it to heirs. Marrett had owned pew forty-five in the third meetinghouse, for which he paid a nine-dollar yearly tax. His father, Amos Marrett Jr., originally purchased the pew for sixty-eight dollars when the church was built in 1794. The pew's location had been prominent—in the front, three pews to the left of the pulpit. Amos Jr. probably inherited the location from his father, Amos. He had served four terms as selectman and fought in the Revolution. Through land purchases Amos Marrett, John's grandfather, had become by 1794 one of the largest landowners in the southeast part of Lexington and became the namesake for Marrett Road.

John Marrett probably inherited the pew location after his father, Amos Jr., died. John was a lifelong bachelor and appeared not to have family to whom to pass the pew property. On the back of John's deed is written a conveyance of the property for $25.50 to George A. Sanborn in 1859, after Marrett's death on August 9, 1858. William Chandler signed it as Marrett's executor.

Eventually, First Parish opened seating to a first come first served basis. But the practice is so accepted that "seating the meetinghouse" still seems curious. Today there are other ways of displaying status.

GRASS

AT AUCTION!

ON THURSDAY, JUNE 25TH,

At 5 o'clock, P. M.,

All the Grass on about seven acres of Land, near the Unitarian Church, in E. Lexington. The above grass is of the

FIRST QUALITY OF

Clover and Herds Grass,

And judged to be two tons to an acre.

ABNER STONE.

P. P. PEIRCE, Auct'r.

East Lexington, June 15th, 1857.

Propeller Job Press, 142 Washington Street, Boston.

ADVERTISEMENT FOR AUCTION OF GRASS, 1857

Little has been written about Lexington's bovine past. But in the first half of the nineteenth century the cow population grew in Lexington at a higher rate than people. In 1810 1,052 people resided in town along with 556 cows. By 1850 the cattle population in Lexington reached its historical peak at 1,419, with the population in people at 1,893. What led to this 255 percent increase in cows in forty years and what were its effects in land use?

During the first part of the nineteenth century, Middlesex County's agricultural economy had been based on grains, grasses and cattle. Hay stood as its largest cash crop. Hauled to Boston via oxcart, and later by barge on the Middlesex Canal, the product was sold at the Hay Market. This area near Boston's North End has kept the name, and is still an open-air market—but for produce. Next to hay, apples of every variety ranked a close second in sales.

Urban areas began to grow in population, shrinking open spaces. For some towns within twenty miles of Boston, such as Lexington, meeting the demand of urban dwellers led farmers to specialize in milk and produce. Lexington's proximity to Boston positioned it well for such commerce. Although as late as 1829 Boston licensed cows for pasture on the Common for five dollars per month, most Bostonians no longer owned a family milk cow. Bostonians and residents of the inner suburbs came to rely on outside delivery. Lexington ranked among the most prominent milk producers in Greater Boston by the early nineteenth century. George O. Smith wrote in 1897 that the town's largest cowherds in 1810 belonged to Reuben Pierce, who had twenty; Amos Marrett, nineteen; Benjamin Wellington, eighteen; Jonas Bridge, fifteen; Phineas Lawrence, ten; and Zeb Adams, ten. In the 1820s Lexington milk producers delivered daily to Boston. According to Smith, Benjamin Wellington was considered the first Lexingtonian with a daily route, followed by Nehemiah Wellington and Samuel Downing. By 1850 the cow population had nearly tripled.

Produce from market gardens also became vital to the farm economy. By the 1860s Lexington began to flourish in growing marketable produce. At the time Lexington was on its way to being among the most productive milk-producing towns in the state. By 1875 it ranked second in the state to Worcester in milk production, a remarkable achievement considering its size. If cows drove this commerce, the most important crop had to be grasses. Feeding cattle with grasses and hay was the foundation of the business.

As cowherds increased in size, the need for grasslands grew apace. According to the 1850 United States Agricultural Census, the size of the Lexington farms ranged from that of Benjamin Reed, who owned 178 acres of improved and 128 acres of unimproved land, to Benjamin Gould's 5-acre farm with 3 improved acres and 2 unimproved. Most Lexington farms were diversified, keeping to the mixed husbandry model of their ancestors. Many grew produce to be transported and sold at the Boston Market while also raising livestock, including swine as well as cows. Each animal might be sold at the Brighton stockyards. But in addition to raising cows for beef, milk cows remained a critical element of the local economy. Farmers either marketed milk on their routes or sold to local milkmen each day for their daily trip into Boston.

The increase in the cattle population created some stresses on pastureland needed to feed livestock. In addition, according to Howard S. Russell in *A Long Deep Furrow: Three Centuries of Farming in New England* farmers had begun to neglect pastures that existed. This led to thin yields. So bad was it in the surrounding area that an 1855 report to the North Middlesex Agricultural Society wryly noted that some animals had to work as hard to find grass in the sparse pasture land as the farmers did during the day. Russell writes that, as a result, some Massachusetts cattle owners drove their cattle to "verdant mountain pastures in New Hampshire and Vermont."

In Lexington the town Common was leased for grazing and hay production for several years. Those without livestock saw profit to be made in selling the grass they had. Shown here is an advertisement in 1857 for an auction of the grass contained on seven acres of land. The landowner is Abner Stone, who may have acquired adjacent land when purchasing Robbins Hall. Auctioning grass and hay probably became a reasonably commonplace occurrence. In the Society archives is an advertisement for an auction for wood as well. In both cases, the high bidder acquired what grew on the lots, but did not purchase the land. The auctioneer for both was a prominent Lexington resident, Peletiah Pierce, who had served as selectman from 1844–46. His name appeared on most of the local auction ads at the time.

In this grass auction, Pierce announced the bids on herd's-grass and clover, the preferred feed for horses and cattle. While the advertisement did not specify the type of clover, farmers commonly sowed herd's-grass with red clover. Early farmers imported both from England at some point. Herd's-grass is saber shaped, coming to a point at the top. Red clover is a weed that can grow as tall as herd's-grass—as much as twenty to thirty inches. The claim of two tons an acre in the advertisement is a good but standard yield. It is likely that the auction's winner would cut the grasses for hay.

After this bovine peak the human population grew in inverse relation to cows. One hundred years later the cow population had shrunk to 250. By 1980 only 18 resided in the town. One resided at Wilson Farm in 1994 as part of an exhibit. Today no cows live in Lexington.

MATTERS OF WAR

From Annapolis Royal March yͤ 8ͭͪ

Ever Honoured father and mother after my Deuty
Rememberd to you and to my Grandfather and
Grandmother: and my Loue to my brothers and
all my frinds = Hoping thees feu lins of my Loue
Will find you in as Good health as J am at
this present Writting: Blessed be god for it

And this is to let you Understand that i Receiued your
Second Letter: and that it is aueery sickly time with us
and we haue Lost aboue Thrascor men that belong
to New England atheir aboue fifty sick
and theur is aboue fifty men sick Jburnæbey cook is
sick: Daniel Loue is sick william hopkins is sick
benjamin Johnson is amost well of his wounds but he
has had a uerey bad swelling upon his thigh aboue
his wounds but we hope he will ore well
Sͬ Charles has Lost as many men out of his Redgement
Coronal whiting has Lost 16 or 17 and he hes 24 men sick
one man Dyed out of our compeney: he blonged to Wobone
his Name was Robert Peirce:
Jonathan Eaton : is is uerey sick
But we hope to se you in alitle time thay that ar strong
but if we stay hear much Longer there will but few of us
se New England but Sͬ Charls sais he will Carrey
us hom as soon as yͤ gouernur Coms: we hope to see
you in a month or six weaks if we liue
for Sir Charles is a wearey of this place and amost
Discorayed and wants to get hom as much as we Do

Out of all New England men thair is but about 40
men fit for Deuty: and their is hardly men enough
to burrey yͤ Dead aloof after yͤ sick for wor we berrey
2 or 3 men Euerey Night; for we berrey them in
men we loos and we berrey them out of yͤ burning
yͤ fule: Down by yͤ water side and we
be low yͤ fort and spread yͤ Ground Leauel ouer them
that they might not be seen

J haue had a uerey Easey time this winter for i haue
been freed from Deuty to Look after bemamin
Johnson and i haue had my health as Well as
Euer i had in my life for which i haue Caus to

HANNANIAH PARKER'S LETTER FROM PORT ROYAL 1711

Letters from a war zone always carry a degree of poignancy, especially from the distance not only of space but also time. The modern-day reader possesses information about the author's fate, unknowable to the correspondent or audience at the time. For Hannaniah Parker two fateful facts stand out. First, Parker's yet to be born nephew, John Parker, no doubt learned about his uncle's fate as part of family lore. Perhaps he even read the letter. For the future captain of the Lexington militia, this and other experiences by Parker relatives in succeeding military actions with the French must have brought into full relief the privations of war. John Parker himself served in the last French war. As he readied his militia to face the British Regulars in 1775, he did so with this understanding. Second, unbeknownst to Hannaniah Parker or those who received the letter, the nineteen-year-old would never return to Lexington. He died and was buried in Nova Scotia.

How he came to be among the New England force under British command in Canada is not known, but he probably enlisted for a bounty. Regardless, Parker found himself at Annapolis Royal (formerly Port Royal) in March 1711, part of an army in desperate straits. Acadia included both Nova Scotia and New Brunswick. As a member of the victorious expedition sent to capture Port Royal, Acadia, from the French, one might think Parker would feel safe. This action was part of Queen Anne's War— one of several between the English and the French in North America before the British expelled French government from the mainland in 1763. Port Royal had long been a particular source of irritation to New

Englanders, as French privateers operated from the port to prey on New England shipping.

After two earlier failed attempts by New England militia to capture this strategically important location, British authorities finally pledged their support with soldiers and officers. Joining with militia from New York and the New England colonies, a formidable force of thirty-six vessels and two thousand men under the command of Colonel Francis Nicholson arrived in Port Royal in October of 1710. Sir Charles Hobby, a knight native to Massachusetts, seconded his command. Colonel Samuel Vetch had been the motivating force behind the invasion, having convinced the British to support it with more than encouragement. Vetch became a senior officer as adjutant general.

Presented with an opponent superior to his 158 very poorly supplied men, Acadian Governor Daniel d'Auger de Subercase surrendered in ten days. In honor of the queen the British renamed their prize Annapolis Royal. Although Samuel Vetch's plan called for the removal of all French Acadians from the surrounding area, British authorities ultimately encouraged them to stay. They had been asked to take an oath of allegiance to the British government, but were allowed to stay despite their refusal. Some did, however, take the British up on their offer of free passage to France.

Parker wrote about six months after the French garrison's evacuation from the fort. But Parker's letter described a victorious army in desperate straits—much of it from disease. Referring to the New Englanders' commander, Parker wrote, "Colonel Whiting has lost 16 or 17 men and he has 24 men sick." One in his company who had died, reported the nineteen-year-old, "belonged to Woburn his name was Robert Pierce."

Although not under fire, Parker worried about the soldiers' fitness. "Out of all New England men thair is but 40 fit for deuty." So debilitated were the British forces that Parker writes, "Thair is hardly enough men to berry ye dead and look after ye sick for we berry two of three men every night." The town below the fort had the largest population of Acadians and the French authorities had begun to secretly urge them to resist, even infiltrating the countryside with French military and neighboring Quebecois. Parker explained that the British buried their dead at night so that the French would not see their diminishing force. Indian unrest contributed to the unease that Parker must have been feeling. French allies, Abenaki and Mikmaq warriors had begun harassing anyone trading with the British.

Parker seemed torn between explaining the dire realities of his circumstances and not wanting to worry his family. He tried to soothe his parents' fears: "I will not have you be discouraged Nor discontented." He claimed that soon he could be home, and that he heard that "thair is men coming from New York to Releave us." Vetch, who had been appointed governor, had left Charles Hobby, his lieutenant governor, in charge while he returned to Boston. Parker must have been told that the return of Vetch would mean he could go home. He predicted that "Sir Charles...will carry up hom as soon as ye Govenor arrives." Speaking for Hobby he added, "he is a wearey of this place and most discouraged." But reality usually won out over protecting his parents from worry. Earlier in the letter he wrote, "We hope to see you in six weaks If we live."

Vetch did return in April. He found that of 450 men with which he began, 116 had died or deserted. In June Vetch ordered 70 officers and men, primarily from New England and very possibly including Hannaniah Parker, on an expedition against the previously mentioned Indians. Abenaki Indians ambushed this force near a stream later renamed Bloody Creek. The battle left 16 dead British soldiers, with the rest taken as captives. Whether Parker died in the battle, became a captive and later died or died in the fort of disease is unknowable today.

When reading the letter one is struck by the pious nature of the man. He begins the letter with the salutation, "ever honoured Father and Mother," hoping they and the rest of the family are well, "blessed by god for it." Bearing an Old Testament name, he represented an earlier generation, still of Cambridge Farms, more connected to his Puritan roots. Edmund Munroe's letter in 1775 had no religious overtones. Then again Parker's religious nature might have been due to personal circumstances. This ancestor of the famous Unitarian minister Theodore Parker might have been more pious due to his family's influence.

After finishing the letter the nineteen-year-old adds a postscript. "But I desire youer prayers for me that I may be kept from sin and sickness beaing in a dangerous place for them booth: for theear is nothing but wickedness carried on hear cursing and Swearing for every man's mouth." This was a typical complaint throughout wars that brought British Regulars and American colonists in close proximity. How difficult it must have been for a devout rural New Englander to be exposed not just to war, but also to Anglican British soldiers. Cursing might have been second nature to career soldiers who enlisted or were pressed into service. Puritan New Englanders must have wondered if God could look favorably on a British victory.

Reading such a letter gives the modern-day reader pause. So many themes seem timeless, found in wars over generations.

Agreeable to the Vote of the Town
I have received by the Hands of the Select
men the Drums provided by the Town for
the Use of the Military Company in the Town
untill the further Orders of the Town
Lexington March 14. 1775   John Parker

ACKNOWLEDGEMENT OF THE RECEIPT OF A DRUM BY MILITIA 1775

A brightly painted drum encased behind glass catches the eye of visitors entering the Hancock Clarke House today. This drum in the hands of the nineteen-year-old William Diamond signaled the Lexington militia assembly as the British Regulars approached the Common. The mystique of an artifact so directly linked to the drama of early morning April 19, 1775, cannot be overstated. The sound from this instrument, to many, signaled the beginning of the American Revolution itself.

Its route from William Diamond's hands to the display in the Hancock Clarke House has several discernable footprints but also some gaps. As the Massachusetts Provincial Government's Committee of Safety, in fall 1774, ordered towns to begin gathering weapons and supplies, town records show that Lexington purchased two snare drums. Pursuant to the Committee's directive, in December Lexington's militia company began drilling on Lexington Common. On March 14, 1775, Captain Parker signed a receipt, shown here, acknowledging his receipt of the drum "by the hand of the selectmen." One of these drums found its way into the hands of William Diamond.

A militia company's drummer performed key functions in addition to sounding the alarm to assemble the men. When the company marched in formation, it kept beat. The fife complemented the drum by supplying the melody side of military field music. During battles the fife and drum aided communication, especially when gunpowder smoke obscured visual signals. Consequently, they both stayed near the commanding officer. The Lexington company's fife player was sixteen-year-old Jonathan Harrington, who lived his entire long life in Lexington, ultimately to be celebrated as the sole survivor of the battle later in life until his death in 1854. When news of the British approach reached Lexington, Captain Parker ordered Diamond to use his drum to reassemble the company. Militia members who lived within hearing distance or had waited in Buckman Tavern assembled "at the beat of the drum." They already had assembled earlier in the night when the British remained quite distant from the town.

Born in Boston in 1755, Diamond (sometimes Dimond) was nineteen years old at the time of the battle, not sixteen, as some have written. Charles Hudson's genealogies date his birth in 1758, leading to the confusion about age. Hudson's date seems to be a mistake. In Boston Diamond apprenticed to a wheelwright and, while there, a British soldier taught him to play the drum. Upon moving to Lexington, this experience made him a natural choice for the position in the company. After the battle Diamond served as a drummer at Bunker Hill and took up arms in other engagements in the war.

It seems that during the war Diamond had moved from Lexington. The town had earlier decided not to pay soldiers who moved away. When he finished his military service in 1781, Diamond successfully sued Lexington for his back pay as a soldier. But he certainly lived in Lexington when he married Rebecca Simonds within the next couple years, since town records show their first child born in 1783. They had seven children, the first six born in Lexington. Lydia, the last, was born in Petersborough, New Hampshire, where the Diamond family moved in 1795. Diamond died there in 1828, his epitaph dating him as seventy-eight at the time. This made him nineteen in April 1775.

Albert Smith, author of *The History of Petersborough, Hillsborough County, New Hampshire*, written in 1876, had benefit of Diamond's recollections, thus certifying his age. *History* paraphrased Diamond's memories of the celebrated battle. When the British began firing, Diamond remembered that he ran, first having to step over a fallen member of the company. He tried to detach himself from the drum to aid his flight. After a struggle he was able to get it over his head, throw the drum over a stone wall and leave it behind just ahead of British bayonets. He procured a musket from a militia member who, according to Smith, "had neither the courage or disposition to use it himself" and went on to Concord with it. There Diamond claims to have seen the British soldier who taught him to drum. Smith writes that the soldier "endeavored to make a sign to [Diamond] of the hostile and deadly intent of the invaders, but was not then understood." Thus, according to Diamond's account, he was not among the reassembled company that engaged the British so effectively during their return to Boston. Possibly, Diamond recovered the drum because his role in the service would be as a drummer.

Ultimately, the drum found its way into the state archives. The drum's disposition after the war until it was placed at the Hancock Clarke House is unknown. This leaves a huge gap in the story. But a letter from the Massachusetts adjutant general's office in 1904 notified the Lexington Historical Society that the state archives had the drum in its possession. Actually, the letter was pursuant to Resolution 1200 of the Massachusetts House of Representatives dated March 13, 1903. This legislative action turned over the drum to the Lexington Historical Society. The adjutant general wrote that "from the year 1863…it had been under my personal observation." He confessed a vested interest in the drum as he was "Lexington born and had pride in that." He further stated that the drum had always been considered the "Lexington Drum," and that "there can be no doubt as to its authenticity."

The fifteen-inch-high, seventeen-inch-wide drum at the Hancock Clarke House shows a brightly painted inscription: "The Battle of Lexington April 19th 1775." Clearly, this commemorative decoration was added after the war. Its appropriateness is clear, since the vibrations emanating from this instrument signaled America's fight for independence.

Lexington Aprill 23, 1775.

I John Parker of lawfull age, and commander of
the militia in Lexington, do testify and declare,
that, on the 19th inst. in the morning about one of
the Clock, being informd that there were a
number of Regular ~~troops~~ officers riding up
& down the road, taking and insulting people,
and also was informed that the ~~find~~ ^Regular^ troops were
on their march from Boston, in order to
take the Province Store at Concord, imme:
diately ordered our militia to meet on the
common in said Lexington, to consult what to
do; and concluded not to be discovered, nor
~~be~~ meddle or make with said Regular Troops
(if they should approach) unless they should insult
or molest us; and upon their sudden approach,
I immediately ordered our militia to disperse
and not to fire; ~~and further he saith not.~~
imediatly said ~~H~~ Troops made their appearance and rushed
furiously ~~to~~ ^us^ fired upon and killed Eight of our party without
Receiving any provocation therefor from us   John Parker

Middx ss April ye 23d 1775
The Above named John Parker appeared and
made solemn oath to the truth of the within deposition
by him subscribed before us.
                                    John Cuming
                                    Jos. Hastings
                              Duncan Ingraham

CAPTAIN JOHN PARKER'S DEPOSITION, 1775

Who fired that first shot on Lexington Common on April 19, 1775, remains today a matter of some academic speculation and much public curiosity. That British Regulars entered Lexington on the way to remove colonial munitions stores in Concord, that they found a militia company of sixty or seventy men commanded by Captain John Parker gathered on the Common and that Major Pitcairn, commander of the advanced guard, had ordered them to disperse is not disputed. How this confrontation erupted into the first battle of the American Revolution, however, remains a mystery.

In the days following the battle, this question was no mere academic exercise. Getting the story right had profound political implications. Today we might call it "spin control." The Massachusetts provincial government believed that to gain the other colonies' support, it needed to convince them that British aggression caused the violence. With Massachusetts's reputation as the most radical of the colonies, with Boston's history of street violence, this task worried the Massachusetts representatives to the Continental Congress soon to be convened. Five days after the battle John Hancock, an occupant of Jonas Clarke's parsonage on April 19 but not an eyewitness to the battle, wrote from Worcester urging the Massachusetts Committee of Safety to send sworn testimony to provide proof that the British fired first. En route to Philadelphia, Hancock knew the Massachusetts representatives need ammunition once there.

The Committee of Safety had already begun to gather eyewitness testimony. Today, manuscript copies of these depositions are scattered among many repositories throughout the Untied States. The Lexington Historical Society owns the critically important manuscript deposition of Captain John Parker. It is among the Society's most significant holdings.

Who was John Parker? Forty-five years of age at the time of the battle, his farm, torn down in 1843, sat near present-day Spring Street. He had served in the final French and Indian War, perhaps with Roger's Rangers. A wheelwright by trade, he had served the town as assessor for a number of years. Parker loved to read, often borrowing books from the largest collection in town—Jonas Clarke's. At the time of the battle, Parker suffered a terminal illness and would die on September 17 later that year of consumption.

Parker reports in his deposition that after being informed of the British approach on April 19 at "about one of the clock" he "immediately ordered our militia to meet on the common of said Lexington, to consult what to do." Requesting input from the company's men was not unusual for a militia officer. The New England militia had a democratic cast to it—officers achieved leadership through election. Parker then implies that the militia's presence on the Common was a defensive show of force, not designed to instigate violence. The decision called for the militia "not to meddle or make with said regular troops if they should approach unless they should insult or molest us." Underscoring the peaceful posture, Parker states that upon the British approach, he "ordered his men to disperse and not to fire." At that point, a shot rang out. Parker claims that the first shot issued from the Regulars as they "rushed furiously, fired upon and killed eight of our party without receiving any provocation threrefor [sic] from us." Contrary to popular belief, his statement does not include, "If they want a war, let it begin here." This statement, attributed to Parker, was a recollection of William Monroe in 1822, causing some historians to believe it more apocryphal than true.

Witnessed by three justices of the peace, Parker signed the deposition on April 23, 1775. A comparison with Parker's account books in the Historical Society archives reveals only the signature in his hand. As with depositions today, his was oral testimony recorded by a scribe. Further evidence can be found at the end of the deposition. While mainly written in the first person, the narrative lapses into the third person with "and further he saith." This is crossed out and a third hand finishes the rest of the deposition, including the key line regarding the instigator of the battle. It would be interesting to know the circumstances that brought a third person to the task at that moment.

Perhaps in the interest of brevity, Parker's version collapsed the timing of events, placing the militia on the Common at 1:00 a.m. with the battle ensuing soon thereafter. Actually, Revere and Dawes arrived at around midnight with the subsequent assembly of the militia ending in dismissal, as the British would not arrive for another five hours.

As a witness, Parker was less than objective. He knew the purpose of the collection of witness testimony. Therefore, these depositions cannot be taken at face value. Nevertheless, simply because those deposed had motive to interpret the event to suit their interests does not mean that their testimonies are not accurate. This is, of course, also true of British reports on the event. Commander of the advanced guard who engaged the militia, Major Pitcairn, commander of the advanced party that engaged the Lexington militia, claimed the shot came from the meetinghouse. He corroborated Parker's account by saying the militia had been dispersing when the shot fired. The testimony of a captive British soldier supporting the colonial view also has problems given his status as a prisoner. And so it goes.

It was not settled then any more than it is now. Despite the concerns of John Adams, Sam Adams and John Hancock regarding the reaction of the other colonies, as they made their way to the Second Continental Congress in Philadelphia, they found complete support. Fortunately, news of the battles in Lexington and Concord preceded them as they traveled. To their pleasure, the countryside met their party with great sympathy and support. The depositions arrived in Philadelphia a little after they did, but were not critical in convincing the Congress of Lexington's victimization.

Another audience, the British public, was persuaded by the depositions according to David Hackett Fischer. Over one hundred of them accompanied by a cover letter written by Dr. Joseph Warren addressed to "Inhabitants of Great Britain" raced across the Atlantic in the American schooner *Quero* to arrive ahead of the British Royal Governor Thomas Gage's report carried in the brig *Sukey*. This allowed the American "spin" on the event to make a first impression. The depositions immediately gained the sympathy of a segment of the British public. Regardless of the source of the first shot in the battle, the first shot in the spin battle definitely issued from the American side.

Lexington April 19th 1775 — the Province of
Massachusetts Debtor to Joseph Fick to going to
Return to Dress one of the kings troops travel three
mills and Dressing: 0   3-6—0

April 19 to Dressing one of kings troops
     at Mr Buckmans in Lexington
                                                        0   2 — 0 0
travel half a mile ————————

April 20th to Dressing Seven of the kings
     troops at Mr Buckmans in
Lexington ~~two~~ two days at one   £   1 — 0 — 0
Shillings pr day pr each ————————

april 20th to going to Lincoln to Dress two
     of kings troops travel three miles   0 — 3 — 6 — 0

april 20th to going to Ebenezer Fipps to dress
     three of the kings troops travel two miles 0 — 3 — 6 — 0

april 23th to going to Cambridge to Dress
     one of the kings troops travel
     five miles ————————   0   4 — 0 — 0

                                   three times
april 2th to Dressings one of kings troops
     at Mr Buckmans in S town
travel half a mile ————————   0   4 — 0 — 0
                                                    0 — 0

Lexington June 6th 177   Errors Excepted
                         Joseph Fick

DR. JOSEPH FISKE'S BILL FOR SERVICES RENDERED, 1775

Submitting expense accounts for reimbursement during the Revolutionary War was not unusual. George Washington, although not taking payment for his service, did ask the Continental Congress to reimburse his expenses. While Paul Revere requested no reimbursement for his famous ride to Lexington, he did ask payment from the Massachusetts Provincial Congress for service later that month "for outdoor activities." Count Lexington's physician, Dr. Joseph Fiske, whose invoice is shown here, among those who submitted such a request for medical services and travel expenses—in this case to treat wounded British Regulars left behind on their return march to Boston.

Three generations of Fiskes—Joseph, his father, Robert, and his son, Joseph Jr.—met the medical needs of Lexington in the eighteenth and early nineteenth centuries. When still a precinct of Cambridge, Robert became the town's first doctor. He eventually moved to the 63 Hancock Street residence beginning in 1732. His son Joseph resided in the same house in 1775. After marrying Elizabeth Stone in 1794, he moved into the East Street home. Ironically, Joseph had traveled to this house for his education as a child. His son, Joseph Jr., carried the family medical tradition into the nineteenth century.

Actually Dr. Fiske was quite familiar with the process of requesting payment from the government for services rendered. Lexington records reveal that town revenue regularly paid Fiske for treating residents. This seemed to have been part of poor relief the town provided widows and other "worthy" poor. If so, it functioned as an early form of Medicaid. But he did not ask town government to pay the bill here.

The expense account submitted to the Massachusetts Provincial Congress details a hectic several days for Dr. Fiske beginning on April 19. His name appears on the muster roll of Captain Parker's company, but he did not make it onto the Common to face the British. At some point he grabbed his medical bag, mounted his horse and rode to attend to the wounded. One can be certain that he treated Patriot wounded also, but since presumably he did not charge the colony for it, no record exists. On the day of the battle, he treated one British soldier in Woburn and one at Buckman Tavern in Lexington. The next day he was back at Buckman dressing the wounds of seven "of the King's troops." Buckman Tavern probably became a central location in which wounded Regulars were housed temporarily. After treating two wounded soldiers in Lincoln, on the return trip on Battle Road (or 2A today) he stopped at his uncle's house. Eighty-four-year-old Ebenezer Fiske's house stood at the junction of Wood Street and Old Massachusetts Avenue. There Dr. Fiske dressed the wounds of two others.

On April 23 and April 26 he reported dressing wounds in Cambridge and Lexington, respectively. It is possible that Fiske had treated these soldiers earlier in the week and wanted to check on their progress. The patient he saw at Buckman Tavern on the April 26 could also have been the individual he first treated on the 19th. This soldier must have survived, as the British Regular buried in the old burial ground died while at the tavern two days after the battle. It is hard to know how many other physicians performed similar duties in the surrounding area, but it is safe to say that Dr. Fiske was one among several.

We do not know the nature of the wounds. The only reference Fiske made regarding the nature of the injuries was that he "dressed" them. He did not report extracting a musket ball. Most were probably flesh gunshot wounds, since the militia did not own bayonets and little close fighting happened that would have involved knives or swords. A British soldier did die at Buckman, however. The eighteenth-century practice for treating a flesh wound involved the physician applying a sticky plaster and bandage, then closing the wound by drawing a strip of cloth together from both ends, to function as a butterfly bandage. Pain was ameliorated with opium administered orally or with a poultice applied to the wound. Gunshot wounds carried the risk of infection as the dirt from the ball as well as clothing entered the body even if the ball did not stay.

British Military Governor Thomas Gage reported 272 casualties, 27 missing among them. Other reports differ slightly. One can surmise that some of the missing died of their wounds, as the Regular who died at Buckman. The wounded at the tavern had to be Regulars wounded on their return trip through Lexington, as no wounded were left behind as they engaged the militia early in the morning. Of course, those wounded who survived became prisoners.

On July 1, 1775, the *Virginia Gazette* reported a prisoner exchange that had happened on June 6. British captured during the Battle of Lexington and Concord were among those returned to Boston. This ended Dr. Fiske's treatment of them. Appropriately, the last date in his expense account dates on June 6. By then the combined militia drawn from local and distant places had laid siege to Boston. The only safe place for Loyalists was Boston. The countryside was under Patriot control.

Dr. Joseph Warren, chairman of the Committee of Safety, and General Israel Putnam, in command of the militia companies who had gathered in response to the alarm, accompanied captured British officers to the exchange point at Charlestown. In two carts the wounded British privates were carried. No doubt Dr. Fiske had treated some of the soldiers. The *Virginia Gazette* describes the meeting as "cordial and affectionate." In exchange, the Patriot prisoners crossed the river by ferry into the arms of their compatriots. The American prisoners were not soldiers, however. Instead they were Boston and Cambridge residents probably arrested for acting against the Crown. According to the *Gazette*, the British officer in charge, Major Moncrief, reported that the British prisoners expressed gratitude for their kind treatment. The privates, the *Gazette* wrote, "who were wounded men, expressed in the strongest terms the grateful sense of tenderness that had been shown them."

If we are to believe this partisan newspaper, Dr. Fiske made his contribution to the good will. It is not known whether he received his requested payment. But if the Massachusetts Provincial Congress responded in a similar manner to such requests as the Continental Congress did their requests, the best he might expect would be a partial payment. No doubt as a physician, Fiske felt a moral obligation to treat those who needed medical help and certainly did not regret the service, regardless of the disposition of his request.

The Battle of Lexington, April 19, 1775. — Plate 1, engraved by Amos Doolittle.

Drawn by Earl & engraved by A.Doolittle in 1775   Re-Engraved by A.Doolittle and J.W.Barber in 1832

BATTLE OF LEXINGTON.

1. Major Pitcairn at the head of the Regular Grenadiers. — 2. The Party who first fired on the Provincials at Lexington.
3. Part of the Provincial Company of Lexington. — 4. Regular Companies on the road to Concord. — 5. The Meeting house.
at Lexington. — 6. The Public Inn.

485

THE DOOLITTLE ENGRAVING 1775

The Battle of Lexington has not lacked for visual representation. It has become an iconographic scene integral to the American tradition. These scenes have varied markedly over the years. Artists of the nineteenth century, removed in time from the 1775 event, submitted romantic scenes, showing the Lexington militia aggressively standing its ground to engage the British, often barring their way. These representations fed an emerging national pride at the expense of accuracy. The only work done by contemporaries, the Doolittle engraving, did not fit within this tradition. If anything it may have underplayed the militia's resistance. In so doing it served the needs of the cause at the time. That the painter who sketched and later painted the scenes that Doolittle engraved held Loyalist sympathies remains the most incongruous part of the story.

Amos Doolittle arrived in Cambridge with Captain Benedict Arnold's Second Company Governor's Guards of New Haven on April 29 in response to what had transpired in Lexington and Concord ten days earlier. His militia company participated in the siege of Boston. A twenty-year-old New Haven silversmith at the time, Doolittle was learning copper plate engraving. During his three-week service, he received leave to travel to Lexington and Concord. Ralph Earl met Doolittle in Lexington. The circumstances that led to their collaboration remain unclear. In March Earl had visited the painter Henry Pelham in Boston. Perhaps he remained in the area into April, or perhaps he returned to New Haven and agreed to meet Doolittle in Lexington upon hearing of the battle.

Twenty-five-year-old Earl was a portrait painter—and a Loyalist—who would soon feel compelled to flee the colonies. Earl drew four landscapes while visiting Lexington and Concord. Of these, plate one portrayed the battle on Lexington Common. To reconstruct the scene as accurately as possible, Doolittle and Earl interviewed participants and observers. Earl's lack of prowess in drawing human figures led Doolittle to pose as a model for several positions. For example, he crouched to fire a musket and posed loading a musket. Later, Earl converted his drawings into an oil painting and Doolittle engraved them on copper plates. In the *Connecticut Journal* on December 13, 1775, four prints were advertised for sale "at the store of Mr. Lockwood, near the college, in New Haven." The price was six shillings for "plain" and eight shillings for a set of colored prints.

As art the scenes are crude, plagued with problems of perspective, making the human figures seem like paper cutouts. Historian Allen French compared them to the Boston Massacre engravings credited to another silversmith, Paul Revere. (Perhaps, while in Boston, Earl received advice from Henry Pelham. He originally drew and engraved the Boston Massacre image only to have Revere copy and re-engrave it.) Aesthetics notwithstanding, the Doolittle engravings remain the only visual representation by artists who walked the ground and talked to participants. The shape and relative locations of the buildings can be relied on for accuracy. The shadows seem consistent with the early morning sunrise when the event took place.

The depiction of the battle, however, does take on some propaganda elements in the tradition of the Boston Massacre engraving. The depositions of participants taken directly after the event reflect a natural motivation to place complete blame for the altercation at the feet of the British. The British response remained unclear and the essential support for Massachusetts among the other colonies also remained unknown. That this was an unprovoked attack on rural farmers needed to be the public storyline. David Hackett Fischer in *Paul Revere's Ride* refers to this as the "myth of wounded innocence." Facts such as the planned advance warning of the British expedition performed by the Committee of Safety and the organization of a complicated alarm system among neighboring towns would not fit this storyline. Therefore, little talk of resistance could be found in the depositions. The engraving reflects this. Virtually everyone is shown leaving the Common upon the order of Captain John Parker. The engraving shows only one militia member not leaving or turning to leave. This probably represents Jonas Parker, who swore to stand his ground even before the confrontation. Depositions taken fifty years later—problematic as recollections fifty years later might be—revealed several more militia than Jonas Parker stood their ground, but most had turned to leave when the shots were fired. Even British Major Pitcairn stated this later.

On the British side the propaganda elements are even more pronounced. The British who rushed onto the Common under Lieutenant Adair had gotten out ahead of their commander, Major Pitcairn. The engraving gives the impression that British Regulars fired on his command. The pose seems like an execution by firing squad and recalls the positioning of British Captain Preston in the Boston Massacre engraving.

Since the original copper engravings have disappeared, any prints published in subsequent years were made from re-engraved plates. In 1832 an aging Amos Doolittle collaborated with John Warner Barber to publish a re-engraved version of the plate. Barber was also a New Haven engraver, a student of Doolittle's and now his colleague. Doolittle drew the sketches for these re-engravings, his first. In the Barber-Doolittle *Battle of Lexington*, shown here as the lower image on the facing page, they used the earlier work as a basis. Barber writes in *Historical Collections of Massachusetts* that the re-engraving was "from original paintings taken on the spot." But it shows a closer, ground-level perspective on a smaller scale.

Other reproductions followed in later years. In 1885 Reverend Edward G. Porter of Lexington's Hancock Church reproduced the original four plates. Book dealer Charles Goodspeed published a re-engraved set of seventy-five much smaller hand-colored prints in 1905. In 1960 Goodspeed published 225 more of these, but at full size. For the bicentennial, the Chicago Historical Society sponsored a limited edition based on the set of originals in their collection. The print shown here seems to be made from an original. Lexington Historical Society does not own an original of plate one.

No one can doubt Amos Doolittle's loyalty to the Patriot cause. For that matter, Ralph Earl left little doubt of his loyalty also—to the British. Ralph Earl's father went in the opposite direction. He served as an officer in the Continental Army after having refused a commission in the British army. The younger Earl, however, refused to serve in the militia and even risked jail for refusing to pay taxes that would support the American cause. He lived in New Haven until he was pressured to leave in April 1777 by a petition that named citizens accused of treason for refusing to serve in the military. This is what makes his participation so interesting. He became an instrument for American propaganda. He left the United States for England in 1778. Before he left he contracted to paint the portrait of Roger Sherman of Connecticut, signer of the Declaration of Independence, Articles of Confederation and Constitution. While in England he studied under Benjamin West and was elected to the Royal Academy. He returned to the United States in 1786 and eventually became an itinerant painter in Connecticut.

Earl could never have predicted that the sketches he produced in Lexington and Concord would become treasured images in the history of a nation he never wanted to exist.

Valey Forge, 12 June. 1778

My Dear,

I Send these lines with the Most Affectionate
love & respects to you & the children wishing they
may find you in Perfect Health & prosperity. — I am
well & in High spirits through divine goodness. —
Lexington men are all well; news we have none except
the Commisioners are arived, from Great Brittain at
Philadelphia in order, the dispute between us & them.
They have Sent a Flag of truce; what they had
to offer, is forwarded to Congress. — The new Establish
of the army is arived in Camp; there is to be a
Large Reducement of officers; but, as it has not taken
place as yet, it is not known who are to be Reduced.
The new arangements are on a Better footing than
they are before. As it is to take place Soon I
will let you know my destiney by Mr Williams
who is in a fair Way to Recover of the Small
Pox; by him I am in Hopes to Send you Some
Money. I Received your letter & a Pair gloves.
I hope to reward you for your kindness to your
Satisfaction. Be kind Enough to let me know
whether you have drawn a Blank or a Prize in
States Lottery. My due respects to all friends
I am my dear your most Affectionate
Husband Edm Munro

EDMUND MUNROE'S LETTER FROM VALLEY FORGE 1777

E-mail appears to be the preferred form of communication between members of the armed forces in Iraq and their families. The speed of cyberspace renders a soldier more accessible to family than letters. Rarely is e-mail lost. During the Revolutionary War, however, "snail" mail offered the best option. Eighteenth-century recipients treasured this contact with a service member at war as much as e-mails are treasured today.

Edmund Munroe wrote his letter on June 12, 1778, from Valley Forge, Pennsylvania, to his wife. At the time, the family probably lived near the juncture of Woburn Street and Lowell Street, in the area of Lexington called Scotland. Before the war, Munroe engaged in the potash business and fur trade, though with limited success. To augment his income, he pastured cattle, farmed and made shoes. Munroe's military experience was extensive. Charles Hudson's genealogies list him as an ensign in Roger's Rangers and lieutenant in the final French and Indian War. Having served for five years in the war, upon return friends and neighbors encouraged him to marry, which he did in 1769. Six years later, he participated in the Battle of Lexington on April 19, 1775.

After his appointment to captain in the Fifteenth Massachusetts Regiment under Colonel Thomas Bigelow in January 1777, Munroe had participated in the Battle of Saratoga before wintering at Valley Forge. Due to his service at Saratoga, he was awarded two candlesticks from the captured British General John Burgoyne's saddlebags. Joining Edmund at Saratoga was William Munroe, his brother and owner of Monroe Tavern.

His wife, the former Rebekah Harrington, probably read the letter to her family and friends. Reading letters to a larger audience served as a form of entertainment in the eighteenth century as well as a way to disseminate news. In time of war, when only a letter could verify a soldier's health, they were most critical to peace of mind. To relieve anxieties in the town, Munroe assured anyone privy to the message that the Lexington men at Valley Forge fared well. An earlier letter had established that Levi Mead and Pompey Blackman, a former slave whose enlistment probably freed him, had been ill. It seems that Mead and Blackman had survived the difficult winter of 1777–78 at Valley Forge.

The winter had proven extremely debilitating. Bereft of food and other supplies, the Americans suffered, while Loyalists entertained the British in Philadelphia. General George Washington complained to the Continental Congress about the "total failure of supplies." So destitute was his army in the winter of 1777–78 that he warned that without Congressional action, "the army must dissolve." The Continental Congress, having been driven out of Philadelphia by the British occupation, finally suggested that Washington commandeer provisions from surrounding towns. He protested that such a practice would spread "disaffection, jealousy and fear among the people." However, left with little alternative, Washington finally consented. By the time Munroe wrote Rebekah, new supplies had arrived in addition to new uniforms and men.

With a reorganization of the army under way, Munroe wrote that "there is to be a large reducement of officers." He wondered if he would be among the officers affected. The letter referred to a Mr. Williams who was to deliver news of the reorganization's outcome to Lexington. Hudson's genealogies do not include a Williams in Lexington during this period. Munroe also mentioned that Williams was in a "fair way" after battling smallpox. It is possible that he was recovering from an inoculation.

Smallpox worried General Washington. When the British evacuated Boston in 1776, they left behind a smallpox epidemic. Washington even hinted that the British had purposely endangered the American army with the disease in a form of biological warfare. (Most British soldiers had acquired immunity in childhood.) Eventually, Washington forbid his soldiers to enter Boston without permission. When smallpox struck the Northern Continental Army and the Ninth North Carolina Regiment, Washington faced a decision.

As he moved toward Valley Forge, he knew Philadelphia to be notoriously smallpox-ridden because the city regulated its inoculations so haphazardly. Controversy still surrounded inoculations, as they clearly presented danger for its recipients. The eighteenth-century process involved planting live smallpox virus pustules into an incision in the arm or hand. The best outcome was a mild case of smallpox followed by immunity for life.

Nevertheless, the patient could die. Finally, as smallpox began to break out at Valley Forge, Washington ordered mass inoculations. Edmund Munroe's experience with smallpox is not clear, but Williams was probably on the road to immunity.

Earlier, Munroe noted the appearance of commissioners "from Great Britain and Philadelphia in order to settle the dispute between us & them." Spurred by the recent alliance after Saratoga between the United States and France, the British made an effort to negotiate a peace. Munroe's prediction about the prospects of peace cannot be discerned by his reference. However, he probably was not optimistic. British condescension and American insistence on nothing short of independence doomed any agreement.

Munroe acknowledges the receipt of Rebekah's letters along with a pair of gloves. Late in the letter, Munroe wondered about his wife's luck in a recent lottery. On May 1, 1778, the General Court voted for a lottery to pay soldiers who had enlisted in the Continental army before April 15, 1777, for a term of at least three years. Munroe was probably referring to it, since the lottery began soon after the legislature's action. Winners of the lottery would earn fifty dollars, to be paid in 1783 with 6 percent interest. Surely, money was an issue at home as Munroe writes of sending Rebekah some, perhaps through the returning Williams.

This was probably the last letter Rebekah Munroe received from her husband. Sixteen days later Edmund Munroe perished in the Battle of Monmouth Courthouse—struck down by the same cannonball that killed his cousin, George Munroe, and took off the leg of Thomas Fox, another Lexingtonian. Whether Rebekah won the lottery is unknown. But the Governor's Council granted Widow Rebecca Munroe 100 pounds on February 6, 1779. However, this was paid in devalued Continental scrip. She continued to get half pay until 1785. Caring for longtime residents who became destitute, often widows, was part of a New England town's communal ethic. Rebekah became dependent on friends and neighbors, and eventually dispersed her children among relatives.

The logistics of returning bodies at the time made the practice prohibitive. Edmund Munroe was buried with the rest of the dead in Freehold, Pennsylvania. The letter remains one of the most valuable documents in the Lexington Historical Society archives.

Massachusetts Militia.

To Mr. *Samuel Swanies*,

YOU being duly enrolled as a Militia Soldier, in the Company under my command, are hereby ordered to appear at the *usual place of parade* in Lexington, on *Tuesday* the 13th day of *Sept*. next at 12 o'clock, ~~in the~~ at noon, armed and equipped as the law directs, for Military duty.

Given at the town of Lexington, this 25th. *day*

of *August*, 1808.

SULLIVAN BURBANK, *Captain.*

MILITIA SUMMONS OF SAMUEL FRANCIS, 1808

Every April 19 Lexington celebrates its militia's proud past. Even after the American Revolution, the new republic that had harbored ancient fears of a standing army continued with the idea of a citizen army. Thus, a decentralized, town-based system served the national defense in the subsequent years of peace. The summons shown here orders Samuel Francis to appear with the militia on September 13, 1808. It gives three weeks advance notice. It is not a request—it is an order.

The law required all Massachusetts towns to field a militia on an appointed day for inspection and drill. Albert Bryant recalls in the *Proceedings in the Lexington Historical Society, Volume II* that for his service this day was the first Tuesday in May. The militia mustered again sometime in the fall for drill. Since this summons set September 13 as the meeting date, it appears to be the fall drill. It stated the inspection would happen in the "usual place of parade." Bryant writes that when summoned for the May inspection of 1832, he went to the designated place at front of the meetinghouse on the Common.

Another part of the order, that the men report "armed and equipped as the law directs," probably referred to the Uniform Militia Act of 1792. This federal legislation created a militia system in which every able-bodied male, age eighteen to forty-five, must participate. It placed the responsibility on the militia members to arm themselves. Although a hardship for those who could not afford the expense, they were nonetheless ordered to serve. Of course, the terms of the order could be interpreted. Once summoned, Bryant discovered that being equipped meant having a "musket, knapsack, cartridge box, priming wire and brush and two flints." Bryant sheepishly remembered only bringing the priming wire, brush and two flints when he appeared for inspection on the appointed day. At roll call each person stood in line for his equipment to be inspected. Bryant stood with what he had. One can only imagine how comical the assembled militia must have looked if many other members brought similar "equipment." To Bryant's relief it began to rain, causing the company to retire to Dudley Tavern, "so it remains an open question whether [his] appearance with [his] equipments would have been very war-like."

The Uniform Militia Act of 1792 aimed to create the capability to fight a war. But President Washington was unhappy with the act, as was President Jefferson. Both favored a system that would separate the younger members, from eighteen to twenty-six years of age. Washington's experience with militia during the Revolution certainly figured into his thinking. He was convinced that a militia composed of young and old together would never be effective.

The rest of Bryant's mustering experience may have been indicative. Once settled in Dudley Tavern, the company voted for a captain. Since everyone elected refused the honor, they elected a woman who lived in the poor house. Some members left in disgust and Bryant writes that that "was the last of the Militia Company of Lexington." But that could not be true. He later dates the last militia assembly to be 1847, with only five members present. The five offered to serve in the Mexican War. No annual militia report was written that year, and the state took the field pieces. Bryant notes that that "closes the existence of all military organizations in this town." He points to a generalized militia-raising problem in surrounding towns. Peace societies had an effect with military matters losing its cache.

But in 1808 one expects a more strident martial interest. British violations of American neutral trading rights on the open seas angered a people not far removed from the previous war against the same nation. Samuel Francis left no record in Lexington. Captain Sullivan Burbank, presumably elected in May, ordered the fall muster. He has a distinguished history in town. Burbank ran a store in East Lexington, probably across the street from Cutler's Tavern, near Arlex Oil today. With his wife Betsey Brown, the first of their six children was born in 1804.

Burbank went on to be a military man of stature. His father Samuel, who served as a lieutenant at Bunker Hill, named his son Sullivan after a general under whom he served. Perhaps the younger Burbank felt an inclination toward the military due to this. At the War of 1812's outset, Burbank received a commission as a lieutenant in the infantry at first as a recruiting officer. But he later saw action in several battles along the Canadian border.

On July 25, 1814, at Lundy's Lane, near Niagara Falls, Ontario, Burbank participated in a famous assault on a British battery under Colonel James Miller. This assault would make the regiment famous as the "I will try" regiment. When asked it he could take the position, Miller replied, "I will try." During the assault Burbank incurred a serious shoulder wound. For his performance, he earned the brevet rank of major.

After the war Burbank remained in the army as captain of the Fifth Regiment of the Infantry, serving along the Canadian frontier in numerous locations. Having risen to the rank of Lieutenant Colonel, he resigned his commission in 1839 at sixty-three years old due to medical problems. He returned to the house at 1415 Massachusetts Avenue for his family in 1831. The house was shared with the family of Captain Phelps by that time.

Militias today have taken on a new importance since many modern militiamen, the National Guard, have seen action in Iraq. No one is summoned, however, as the National Guard is all volunteer.

VIEW OF THE MONUMENT AND BATTLE-GROUND, AT LEXINGTON, MASS.

LEXINGTON SCENE WOODCUT 1851

When someone refers to Lexington's Revolutionary War monument, the Captain Parker statue elicits the first image in many minds. But for over one hundred years the monument that represented the fallen militia in the Battle of Lexington sat atop a little hill on the Massachusetts Avenue side of the Common. Dedicated in 1799, this obelisk is probably the nation's oldest Revolutionary War memorial. Frequently, nineteenth-century woodcuts and engravings make it the centerpiece when depicting a typical Lexington scene. Such was the case with the woodcut shown here, which appeared in Gleason's Pictorial Drawing-Room Companion in 1851. For several generations, however, Lexingtonians were not completely satisfied with this commemoration of the town's most famous event.

The *Gleason's Companion* was one of many popular illustrated weekly newspapers, such as *Harper's Illustrated Weekly* and *Frank Leslie's Illustrated Newspaper*. These graphic newspapers became very popular in mid-century, continuing until photographs replaced the illustrations. The articles were copiously illustrated using woodcuts or steel plate engravings, covering subjects such as war, politics, travel and science.

This woodcut shows people, probably visitors, viewing the monument while standing on the Massachusetts Avenue side. A fence did enclose the Common at the time. Constructed in 1830, a wooden fence facilitated renting the space for pasturing. In 1846 a split stone fence, shown here, replaced the earlier fence. In the woodcut's background Buckman Tavern stands to the right, while the Lexington Academy/Normal School building peeks out from the left. Jonathan Harrington's house, complete with a barn, since torn down, stands on the far right. Perspective may account for the monument appearing slightly oversized.

Interest in a Lexington monument began a few years after the Revolutionary War ended. Residents began to believe that the events of April 19, 1775, warranted an appropriate commemoration. Understanding the event's larger significance, the town meeting sought funds from the state. In 1796 Joseph Simonds, writing for the town, petitioned the General Court to fund such a memorial. In a resolution passed February 28, 1797, the state legislature allocated $200 for a monument "to be erected on the ground where the said citizens were slain." In 1798 the legislature added an additional $200. Appropriately, Jonas Clarke wrote the inscription, engraved on a marble tablet facing the people standing in the woodcut. Schoolhouse hill, an elevated part of the Common where the town schoolhouse had sat, was selected as the site.

In addition to the state funds, voluntary town labor graded the hill for the monument's placement. Town funds also supplied food and drink for the volunteers—$19.62 to the nearby Dudley Tavern. To position the granite monument, the town meeting appropriated $87.63 for ropes, later recouping some of it by selling the ropes for $49.50. On the day of dedication, July 4, 1799, $50 from town coffers paid for the celebration's refreshments, especially rum from the taverns.

Why the design of the monument? Later nineteenth-century monuments such as the Washington Monument and Bunker Hill also took the form of obelisks, albeit much larger. Historians often refer to these larger monuments as examples of the Egyptian revival that influenced art and architecture in the United States in the 1840s and 1850s. Spurred by Napoleon's Egyptian campaign in 1798–99 with the resultant coverage from *The National Intelligencer*, this revival caught on in Europe earlier in the nineteenth century. Later it migrated to the United States. But the earlier Lexington monument predated the American version of the Egyptian revival. Egyptian influence, nonetheless, had been present in the United States even before the revival, as the new nation looked to ancient symbols in its search for identity.

Furthermore, obelisks had become accepted funerary symbols, often considered the symbol of eternal life. The inscription on the monument states that the monument is dedicated to the eight men "who fell on this field, the first victims of British Tyranny and Oppression." While at the time of dedication no bodies lay below, that would change.

Sixty years after the battle, on April 19, 1835, the remains of the eight slain militia, seven from Lexington and one from Woburn, were re-interred in a tomb near the monument's base. In 1775 the bodies had been hastily buried in a common grave near the graveyard. With their remains, several other items were placed in the sarcophagus: Elias Phinney's *History of the Battle of Lexington*, a sketch and order of the day's exercises, the names of the president, the acting governor and clergymen of Lexington. As part of an elaborate dedication ceremony, thirteen surviving members of Captain Parker's company shared the podium with keynote speaker Edward Everett, whose oration would later precede Abraham Lincoln's dedication at Gettysburg. In Lexington Everett made a speech of similar length—two hours.

But as the nineteenth century progressed, larger monuments began to crop up in other places as the new country began to shape its collective memory. Prominent Lexington residents began to believe their monument unworthy of the event's stature. In 1850 Benson J. Lossing, having visited Lexington, wrote in the *Pictorial Field Book of the Revolution* that the monument he visited was not "graceful" and in fact was "dumpy." More important than his opinion, he noted that "the people [in Lexington] were dissatisfied by it." It seems the town was suffering from monument envy. Consequently, on April 22, 1850, the Lexington Monument Association was incorporated, with the battle's last survivor, Jonathan Harrington, as president. It dedicated itself to raising money for a "more fitting" monument for the Common. The Bunker Hill Association's success in raising funds for its monument had been duly noted and Lexington hoped to emulate it. Little happened for eight years. But in 1858 Charles Hudson, the town historian and later the author of *History of Lexington*, became the moving force behind the Lexington Association. He went national with the campaign.

Edward Everett agreed to become president. In a national fundraising letter in 1859, Everett describes the proposed monument. "The figure of a Minute-Man" would stand on a "lofty pedestal of granite." The statue would be "bronze and of colossal size." The plan called for a sixty-foot statue. Hammat Billings, with his huge Plymouth monument still in the planning stages, had designed it.

Charter members in the Association received beautifully engraved certificates for a donation of $2,000. Corrected for inflation this would equal $40,000 in today's money. These certificates were purchased by people of means nationwide. How many were sold remains unknown, but the Association spent a great deal of the money on promotion. Events and sentiment, however, eventually conspired against the Association. The beginning of the Civil War dampened support for the project. This spark never reignited. Many residents began to believe that the present monument was just fine and shifted their focus to commemorating the

Civil War sacrifices. Mrs. Maria Cary, who had promised $4,000 to the Monument Association, used the money instead to fund statues of a militiaman of the Revolution and a soldier of the Civil War, placed in the memorial room in the new town hall in 1871.

It is hard to imagine a sixty-foot monument looming over one's approach to the Common. Perhaps we would have grown to love it, thought it perfectly normal and appropriate. Instead the nation's oldest Revolutionary War monument remains in the place it began, humble but a survivor.

BIBLIOGRAPHY

Appleby, Joyce. *Inheriting the Revolution: The First Generation of Americans.* Cambridge, MA: Belknap, 2000.

Benes, Peter. "Decorated Family Registers in New England." In *The Art of Family: Genealogical Artifacts in New England*, edited by D. Benton Simons and Peter Benes, 201–221. Boston: New England Genealogical Society, 2002.

Board of Selectmen. Manuscript minutes, 1713 to 1840. Lexington Historical Society Archives, Lexington, MA.

Brown, Richard D. *Knowledge is Power: The Diffusion of Information in Early America, 1700–1865.* New York: Oxford University Press, 1989.

Canavan, Michael. *The Canavan Papers.* Unpublished.

Carrik, Alice van Leer. *A history of American silhouettes; a collector's guide, 1790–1840.* Rutland, VT: C.E. Tuttle, 1968.

Damase, Jacques. *Carriages.* Translated by William Mitchell. New York: Putnam, 1968.

Dinkin, Robert J. "Seating the Meeting House in Early Massachusetts." *New England Quarterly* 43 (1970): 450–64.

BIBLIOGRAPHY

Faragher, John Mack. *A Great and Noble Scheme: The Tragic Story of the Expulsion of the French Acadians From Their Native Homeland*. New York: Norton, 2005.

Fenn, Elizabeth Anne. *Pox Americana: The Great Smallpox Epidemic of 1775–1782*. New York: Hill and Wang, 2002.

Fischer, David Hackett. *Albion's Seed*. New York: Oxford University Press, 1989.

———. *Liberty and Freedom*. New York: Oxford University Press, 2005.

———. *Paul Revere's Ride*. New York: Oxford University Press, 1994.

French, Allen. *The Day of Concord and Lexington*. 1925. Reprint, Eastern National Park and Monument Association, 1964.

Galvin, John R. *The Minutemen*. Washington, D.C.: Brassey's, 1989.

Goldstein, Warren. *Playing for Keeps: A History of Early Baseball*. Ithaca, NY: Cornell University Press, 1989.

Green, Evarts, and Virginia Harrington. *American Population Before the Federal Census of 1790*. New York: Columbia University Press, 1932. Reprint, Gloucester, MA: Peter Smith, 1969.

Greene, Lorenzo Johnston. *The Negro In Colonial New England*. New York: Atheneum, 1971.

Gross, Robert A. *The Minutemen and Their World*. New York: Hill and Wang, 1976.

Hinkle, Alice. *Prince Estabrook Slave and Soldier*. Lexington, MA: Pleasant Mountain Press, 2001.

Hudson, Charles. *History of Lexington, Massachusetts, Vols. I and II*. Boston: Houghton Mifflin, 1913.

Kammen, Michael. *Mystic Chords of Memory: The Transformation of Tradition in American Culture*. New York: Knopf, 1991.

Kellerer, Tom. "Baseball before 1860." Papers and articles found at Sturbridge Village. http://www.osv.org/

BIBLIOGRAPHY

Kollen, Richard P. *Lexington: From Liberty's Birthplace to Progressive Suburb.* Charleston, SC: Arcadia, 2004.

Kornhauser, Elizabeth Mankin, Richard L. Bushman, Stephen H. Kornhauser, and Aileen Ribeiro. *Ralph Earl: The Face of the Young Republic.* New Haven: Yale University Press, 1991.

Lahikainen, Dean T. *Lexington Portraits: A Catalogue of American Portraits at the Lexington Historical Society, 1734–1884.* Lexington, MA: Lexington Historical Society, 1977.

Larkin, Jack. "Remembering the Sabbath: Worship in New England Meetinghouses." Papers and articles found at Sturbridge Village. http://www.osv.org/

—————. *The Reshaping of Everyday Life: 1790–1840.* New York: Harper, 1989.

Lexington Historical Society. *Proceedings Vol. 1–4.* Lexington, MA: Lexington Historical Society, 1889–1912.

Lossing, Benson John. *The pictorial field-book of the Revolution; or, Illustrations, by pen and pencil, of the history, biography, scenery, relics, and traditions of the War for Independence.* New York: Harper and Brother, 1860.

Mansur, Ina. *A New England Church: 1730–1834.* Freeport, ME: Bond Wheelwright, 1974.

Menand, Catherine S. "The Things That Were Caesar's: Tax Collecting in Eighteenth-Century Boston." *Massachusetts Historical Review* I (1999): 49–78.

Peterson, Mark. "Civil Unions on a Hill." *Common-Place* 4, no. 3 (April 2004): www.common-Place.org/vol-04/no-03/talk/

Pierce, Cyrus, and Mary Swift. *The First State Normal School in America: The Journals.* Cambridge: Harvard University Press, 1928.

Piersen, William D. *Black Yankees: The Development of an Afro-American Subculture in Eighteenth-Century New England.* Amherst: University of Massachusetts Press, 1988.

Pullen, Doris L., and Donald B. Cobb. *The Celebration of April the Nineteenth From 1776 to 1960 In Lexington Massachusetts.* Lexington, MA: Town Celebrations Committee, 1960.

BIBLIOGRAPHY

"Ralph Earl," Biographies Early American Artists, Worcester Art Museum. http://www.worcesterart.org/Collection/Early_American/Artists/earl_r/biography/content.html

Reinhardt, Elizabeth, and Anne Grady. "Asher Benjamin in East Lexington, Massachusetts." *Old-time New England* LXVII (1977): 23–35.

Richards. Leonard. *Shays' Rebellion.* Philadelphia: University of Pennsylvania Press, 2003.

Rothman, David J. *The Discovery of the Asylum: Social Order and Disorder in the New Republic.* New York: Aldine de Gruyter, 1990.

Russell, Howard S. *A Long Deep Furrow: Three Centuries of Farming in New England.* Hanover, NH: University Press of New England, 1976.

Ryan, D. Michael. "Doolittle Engraves April 19th for Prosperity." *Concord Magazine,* June/July 1999. www.concordma.com/magazine/jujuly99/doolittle.html

Seasholes, Nancy, and Anne Grady. *Comprehensive Cultural Resources Survey of Lexington, Massachusetts, Book 1.* Lexington, MA: Town of Lexington, 1976.

Sileo, Tom. *Historical Guide to Open Space in Lexington.* Acton, MA: Thomas P. Sileo, 1995.

Smith, Albert. *History of the Town of Petersborough, Hillsborough County, New Hampshire.* Boston: Cornell University Press, 1876.

Special collections. Concord Library, Concord, MA.

Tourtellot, Arthur Bernon. *William Diamond's Drum: The Beginning of the War of the American Revolution.* New York: Doubleday & Company, 1959.

Twombly, Robert C., and Richard H. Moore. "Black Puritan: The Negro in Seventeenth Century Massachusetts." *William and Mary Quarterly* XXIV, no. 2: 224–42

U.S. Agricultural census 1850, 1860, 1870.

Whitehill, Walter Muir. *Amos Doolittle's Engravings of the Battles of Lexington and Concord.* Chicago: R.R. Donnelley, 1975.

BIBLIOGRAPHY

Wood, Joseph S. *The New England Village*. Baltimore: Johns Hopkins University Press, 1997.

Worthen, Edwin. *Calendar History of Lexington, Massachusetts: 1620–1946*. Lexington, MA: Savings Bank, 1946.

———. *Tracing the Past in Lexington, Massachusetts*. New York: Vantage Press, 1998.

ABOUT THE AUTHOR

 Richard Kollen is the archivist for the Lexington Historical Society and teaches at Lexington High School, Northeastern University and Middlesex Community College. He has written a history of Lexington entitled *Lexington: From Liberty's Birthplace to Progressive Suburb.*